FORTUNE-T

A practical introductory guide to the ancient science of astrology

In the same series:

FORTUNE-TELLING BY CRYSTALS AND SEMIPRECIOUS STONES
  Ursula Markham
FORTUNE-TELLING BY DICE
  David and Julia Line
FORTUNE-TELLING BY MAH JONGG
  Derek Walters
FORTUNE-TELLING BY PALMISTRY
  Rodney Davies
FORTUNE-TELLING BY PLAYING CARDS
  Nerys Dee
FORTUNE-TELLING BY RUNES
  David and Julia Line
FORTUNE-TELLING BY TAROT CARDS
  Sasha Fenton
FORTUNE-TELLING WITH NUMBERS
  Rodney Davies

FORTUNE-TELLING BY ASTROLOGY

The History and Practice of Divination by the Stars

RODNEY DAVIES

THE AQUARIAN PRESS

To my son James

First published 1988

© Rodney Davies 1988

British Library Cataloguing in Publication Data

Davies, Rodney
Fortune-telling by astrology.
1. Astrological predictions. Horoscopes
I. Title
133.5'4

ISBN 0-85030-680-9

*The Aquarian Press is part of the Thorsons Publishing Group,
Wellingborough, Northamptonshire, NN8 2RQ, England*

Printed in Great Britain by Biddles Limited, Guildford, Surrey

3   5   7   9   10   8   6   4   2

CONTENTS

Here will I lie, while these long branches sway,
And you fair stars that crown a happy day
Go in and out as if at merry play,
Who am no more so all forlorn,
As when it seem'd far better to be born
To labour and the mattock-harden'd hand,
Than nursed at ease and brought to understand
A sad astrology, the boundless plan
That makes you tyrants in your iron skies,
Innumerable, pitiless, passionless eyes,
Cold fires, yet with power to burn and brand
His nothingness into man.

From *Maud* by Alfred Tennyson

INTRODUCTION

'What powerful star shined at this man's nativity,
And bless'd his homely cradle with full glory?'

Maximinian in *The Prophetess* by Beaumont and Fletcher.

Astrology is an ancient method of divination, whereby the placement of
certain celestial bodies is interpreted in terms of human character and
destiny. The word itself is built up from the Greek *astron*, or 'star', and
logia, meaning 'the study of', and thus means 'star study'. But it should
really be called 'astromancy' or 'star divination', as astrology has long
ceased to be concerned with the actual observation of celestial objects
and events, which is nowadays the province of astronomy. But it should
not be forgotten that the earliest 'star studiers' both monitored the
movements of such heavenly objects as the Sun and the Moon, which
eventually enabled them to construct accurate calendars and to predict
eclipses, while at the same time using their findings to apparently determine the will of the gods or, in other words, the destiny of themselves
and their fellows. Hence early astrology was practical from both a
utilitarian and a metaphysical point of view.

There can be no doubt that astrology is the best known and most popular of the various methods of prediction that have come down to us
through the ages. Modern man's fascination with it can be judged from
the number of newspapers and magazines that publish, and the radio and
television stations that broadcast, astrological predictions — and by the
fact that practically everyone knows what 'Sun sign' he or she was 'born
under'. This interest is not, however, approved of by scientists, who
regard astrology as superstitious nonsense, even though it attracted the
sympathetic attention of such luminaries as Aristotle, Copernicus,
Galileo, Tycho Brahe, Johan Kepler and Isaac Newton. Indeed, it was

Newton who uttered astrology's most famous reply to ill-informed criticism, when he rounded on Edmond Halley, the astronomer, who had protested at his defence of astrology, and said, 'I have studied the subject, Mr Halley, and you have not'.

But while astrology is popular, it is generally regarded as an enigmatic and difficult pursuit, one that is best left to the experts. This notion derives from the fact that in order to construct a birth chart, which is a diagrammatic representation of the sky at the moment of someone's birth, the astrologer must do some mathematics and consult various tables, while the chart's interpretation — the most important part — requires an understanding of the properties of the planets and those of the different zodiac signs and houses in which they lie, and also of the angular relationships between the planets. And because this is a lengthy and rather technical business, it is not surprising that many people feel that they lack the wherewithal to cope with it.

This is why I have approached the subject from an oblique and non-technical angle, while at the same time covering its main points, as well as some interesting, yet little known, aspects of the art. The book is therefore an introduction to the practice of astrology, and will allow those who have no mathematical skills to learn quite a lot about themselves and their fate — painlessly and, hopefully, enjoyably.

1

ASTROLOGY'S BEGINNINGS

We that are of purer fire,
Imitate the starry quire,
Who in their nightly watchful spheres,
Lead in swift round the months and years.

From *Comus* by John Milton

The world's first civilization arose at the start of the third millennium BC on the lower reaches of the Tigris and Euphrates rivers, in what is now Iraq. The people there, who called their land Sumer, quite suddenly and inexplicably began to build large, walled cities out of sundried mud bricks on the banks of the two great rivers, and dug an extensive network of irrigation canals that allowed them to grow, in the fertile alluvial soil, an abundance of wheat, barley, millet and sesame, whose surplus they traded with their neighbours for the wood, metal and stone that the region lacked. In time, the growing wealth of the cities led to the formation of a non-productive priestly class, who had both the opportunity and the incentive to study the stars. These men were the first astrologers.

The Sumerians worshipped hundreds of gods, and were as a whole a most religious race. Yet their dieties were not accorded equal rank, a small group of the oldest gods and goddesses being the most powerful and important, while the remainder consisted of relatively minor divinities and spirits.

They believed that in the beginning the sky-god An and the earth-goddess Ki had been simultaneously generated from Nammu, the primaeval ocean, locked in a cosmic embrace. From their union was born the air-god Enlil, who forced the copulating couple apart to create the cosmos as we know it. These three deities, An, Ki and Enlil — the sky, the earth and the air — together formed the supreme triad. But such divine procreation did not stop with the birth of Enlil, or 'Lord Air', because he soon fell in love with and ravished Ninlil, or 'Lady Air', who became pregnant, although the texts so far discovered have not revealed Ninlil's origin.

In due course, Ninlil gave birth to Nanna, the Moon-god, who in turn fathered on his wife Ningal the Sun-god Utu and Inanna, the goddess of the bright 'star' we call Venus. Together Nanna, Utu and Inanna made up the divine astral triad, which was second only in importance to that of An, Ki and Enlil, but more loved by men as the deities concerned were responsible for driving away the darkness with their light.

But while the Moon, the Sun and the planet Venus were regarded as gods by the Sumerians, they were also pictured as having, like the other deities, both a human form and human emotions and needs. Indeed, it was the failure of Lahar, the cattle-god, and Ashnan, the grain-goddess, to provide food for the great gods — they fell asleep on the job — that prompted Nammu and Ninmah, the goddess of birth, to create human beings from clay, for the sole purpose of feeding them with offerings of grain and sacrificed animals. This is why the Sumerians believed themselves to be the servants of the gods.

The Sumerians imagined that the earth was a flat disc that floated upon an ocean of fresh or 'sweet' water, on whose peripheral mountains rested the sky or firmament. The Moon-god Nanna was thought to float through the heavens in a boat, while Utu, the Sun-god, apparently rode through them in a chariot. Under the earth was a vast, dark cavern surrounded by seven walls, the 'land of no return', which served as a repository for the souls of the dead. This gloomy underworld was presided over by Ereshkigal, Inanna's sister, and her husband Nergal, the god of war and pestilence.

Each of the 13 principal Sumerian cities had its own patron-god or goddess, who both owned the city and looked after its interests. Thus Nanna was the patron-god of Ur, Utu of Sippur and Larsa, and Inanna of Uruk. A city's king was believed to have been set upon his throne by the patron-god, whose earthly representative he therefore was. And when one city made war against another, it was said that just as the two armies fought, so too did their patron-gods.

As one city's fortunes in war improved, this naturally reflected the increasing power of its patron-god. Such success accounted for the growing prominence of Ningirsu, the patron-god of Lagash, in the middle of the third millennium BC, when the army of Lagash successively defeated those of Ur, Uruk and Umma. This led to Ningirsu being called the 'champion of the celestial gods' and to his identification with the constellation of Orion.

In about 2400 BC the cities of Sumer received a sharp shock when they were invaded by their neighbours, the Akkadians. Akkad lay to the north-west of Sumer, in what is now central Iraq, and while its civilization was identical to that of Sumer, its people spoke a Semitic tongue. The man who orchestrated the invasion was the great Sargon, the King of Kish, whose successful military action established the Akkadian empire and which in turn mirrored the dominance in heaven of Sargon's guardian deity, the goddess Inanna.

Sargon's reign lasted for 55 years and the Akkadian empire for a further one hundred years. Its downfall occurred in 2230 BC, when the ruler Shar-kali-sharri was overthrown in a palace revolution. Several Sumerian cities then broke free from Akkadian rule, and the Akkadian armies were defeated by outside invaders, the chief of whom were the Guti from the Zagros mountains in the east. A period of warfare and uncertainty followed, which led to a new phase of Sumerian ascendancy when Ur-Nammu (ruled 2113-2096 BC), the king of Ur, overthrew his rival Utu-hegal, the king of Uruk, and subsequently became the ruler of both Sumer and Akkad.

The name Ur-nammu means 'man of the goddess Nammu' and reveals that the king was dedicated to Nammu at birth, who was therefore his tutelary deity. We have already seen how Nammu, the primaeval ocean, not only generated the sky-god An and the earth-goddess Ki, but also helped create mankind. Hence it was wholly appropriate that a king named for her should initiate the Sumerian renaissance.

Ur-Nammu quickly organized the digging out of the silted-up irrigation canals, restored farming and thereby trade, promoted the arts, and, fully conscious that he was the gods' representative on earth, began the long task of rebuilding the damaged temples. This latter work led him to construct massive pyramidal stage-towers known as *ziqqurats* (or ziggurats), which rose up above the surrounding city buildings like minature mountains. Indeed, it was the erection of the ziqqurat at Bab-Ilim or Babylon that is referred to in the Bible: 'And they said, Go to, let us build a city and a tower, whose top may reach unto heaven; and let us make a name, lest we be scattered abroad upon the face of the whole earth . . . Therefore is the name of it called Babel' (Genesis 11:4).

The largest ziqqurats were about 150 feet in height and their construction must have entailed an enormous amount of co-ordinated effort. It is not yet known what purpose they served, although it has been suggested that they were astronomical observatories. However, it is more likely that, thrusting as they did so high into the air, the summits of the ziqqurats acted as terrestrial points onto which the city's god or goddess could descend to be among, so to speak, his or her people. This idea is supported by the Greek historian Herodotus, who wrote of the ziqqurat of Babylon:

> On the summit of the topmost tower stands a great temple with a fine couch in it, richly covered, and a golden table beside it. The shrine contains no image, and no-one spends the night there except (if we may believe the Chaldeans who are the priests of Bel or Enlil) one Assyrian woman, all alone, whoever it may be that the god has chosen. The Chaldeans also say — though I do not believe them — that the god enters the temple in person and take his rest upon the bed.

Ur-Nammu was killed in battle in 2096 BC and was succeeded by his son Shulgi, who ruled Sumer and Akkad until his death in 2048 BC. He continued with the work of temple reconstruction and ziqqurat building that his father had begun, and was worshipped as a god in his own lifetime. He in turn was succeeded by his son Amar-Sin, who somewhat immodestly called himself 'the god who gives life to his country', and who, at his death nine years later, was replaced by his brother Shu-Sin (ruled 2038–2030 BC). Shu-Sin was followed by his son, the unfortunate Ibbi-Sin, who almost immediately faced an internal insurrection and, shortly thereafter, an invasion by the Amorites, a nomadic group of people from the Syrian desert, whom the Sumerians regarded as being little more than uncouth savages. After a long and difficult campaign Ibbi-Sin and his army managed to defeat the Amorites, but no sooner had that been accomplished than Sumer and Akkad were again attacked, this time from the east, by the Elamites, who inhabited what is today Iran. In 2006 BC the Elamites beseiged and eventually sacked Ur, Ibbi-Sin's capital city, and captured the monarch himself. The Sumerian and Akkadian empire was thereby destroyed, its people killed or left to starve, and its once-mighty cities put to the torch. From that time on foreigners would rule over the land.

It was during this long and eventful period, which occupied almost the whole of the third millennium BC, that several important astronomical observations were made and the theory of astral influence developed. We must now turn our attention to what these findings and ideas were, how they were used, and how they were incorporated into the Sumerians's framework of religious beliefs.

The observation of the stars by the Sumerians was essentially a religious act. Indeed, the sky itself was considered to be a god, although An, the sky-god, was thought to reside in its very uppermost portion, which was known as the 'sky of An'. Enlil, the air-god, whose anger was expressed as the hurricane and the storm-wind, likewise had a palace in the sky and also a particular strip of stars — Enlil's Way — along which he was believed to walk. The stars themselves were regarded as minor deities and were called the 'soldiers of An'. And through the sky moved the gods of the great astral triad — Nanna, the Moon; Utu, the Sun; and Inanna, the planet Venus. Thus when a Sumerian or an Akkadian looked at the sky, he gazed up at the gods and was filled with wonder and awe. For each visible object was associated with an invisible spiritual being, who knew each man's thoughts, judged his actions, and gave him blessings or sent him tribulations.

By regularly observing the sky and by keeping detailed records of what they saw — the Sumerians wrote in a cuneiform script on clay tablets — it was discovered at an early date that the Moon travelled through the sky along a fixed path, which we know today as the *ecliptic*, and that this was also taken by certain wandering stars, so-called because they sometimes reversed their direction of movement. These 'wanderers' or, to use the Greek term, *planetes* (hence 'planets') were thus distinguished from the other stars, which kept the same positions relative to one another. And of these the most important was the planet Venus, with which the Sumerians identified their goddess Inanna. Indeed, it was Venus' close association with the Sun that led the Sumerians to suppose that Inanna was both the sister and wife of Utu, the Sun-god. The other visible planets — Mercury, Mars, Jupiter and Saturn — were given scant attention by the Sumerians, although by Babylonian times Mars had become linked with their war-god Nergal, Mercury with Nebo, the god of intelligence, Jupiter with Marduk, Nebo's father, and Saturn with Ninib, the god of wisdom and old age.

Nanna, the Moon-god, had his chief temple at Ur and was represented in temple carvings as an old man with a long beard. The Moon's regular cycle of growth and diminution, made up of a waxing phase when it increases in size from New to Full, which takes 14½ days, and a waning phase of the same length, the two together constituting one 'moonth' or month, gave the Sumerians their principal measure of time, which is why they regarded Nanna as the measurer of time. The Moon's regular transformations likewise suggested mystery and, in turn, wisdom — thus Nanna was called 'He whose deep heart no god can penetrate'. And because the Moon gave light to the night, Nanna was the enemy of the criminal and the evil–doer. The Moon's occasional eclipsing, which caused great consternation among the Sumerians, was thought to be brought about by the evil spirits of darkness ganging up with Nanna's two children, Utu and Inanna, to temporarily deprive the god of his light. Each night of its cycle, the Moon was said to navigate its way through the stars in a *quffah*, a circular boat rather like a large coracle. Nanna's wife was Ningal, the 'great lady'.

Utu, the Sun-god, ascended into the sky each morning through a gate in the Mountain of the East, riding in a chariot driven by his coachman Bunene, to bring light to the world. He not only conquered the night, but also winter, and was therefore imbued with courage, energy and daring. And because he, like Nanna, chased away thieves, assassins and all those who hoped to take advantage of the night for evil purposes, while at the same time seeing all from his vantage point in heaven, he was considered to be the god of justice. Utu was also the god of divination, who could reveal the will of the gods and make known the future through his soothsayers. In fact the chief centre of divination in Sumerian times was Sippur, where Utu had his most important temple. He was also the patron-god of Larsa and, later, of Babylon.

The last of the three great astral deities was Inanna, the sister and wife of Utu, who was identified with the planet we call Venus. Titled 'the Queen of Heaven', Inanna was said to have once stolen the 'tablets of destiny' from Enki, the god of wisdom, whose property they were. Inanna then rode through the sky in her boat to Uruk, the city of which she was the patron-goddess, taking the tablets with her, and in this way brought the blessings of civilization to mankind. Yet we would be wrong in thinking that Inanna was generally regarded by the Sumerians as a beneficent goddess. In fact she was originally a goddess of war, who through her actions helped populate the underworld, which was presided over by her sister Ereshkigal, the goddess of death. It was a bad omen when Venus could be seen at sunset, when the planet was called the 'Star of Lamentation'. Later, however, Inanna became a love goddess — she was known to the Greeks as Aphrodite and to the Romans as Venus — who prompted desire in men's hearts and caused animals to mate. Yet while Inanna was held to have had many lovers, those who succumbed to her charms lived to regret it, just as she once ordered her demons to carry off her husband Dumuzi, the god of the harvest, to the underworld when he refused to kneel before her. Inanna and Dumuzi were both the patron deities of Uruk, a city which stood, like Ur and Larsa, on the banks of the Euphrates.

These three astral deities together governed the most important aspects of an individual's life. They drove away the darkness and the evil spirits that accompanied it, including those responsible for sickness and madness, and they punished the wrongdoer; they regulated the growth of crops and marked the passage of time; they gave good luck in love and war; they gave wisdom; and they determined how and when death would occur.

The Sumerians were exposed to exactly the same upturns and downturns of fortune that we are: they knew joy and sorrow, love and hate, health and disease, birth and death, friendship and loneliness, and so forth. But while they believed that the gods rewarded the humble and righteous and punished those who were not, they too often found that the good suffered and the wicked prospered, which led one perplexed poet to ask:

Who knows the will of the gods in heaven?
Who understands the plan of the underworld gods?
Where have mortals learnt the way of a god?
He who was alive yesterday is dead today.
For a minute he was dejected, suddenly he is exuberant.
One moment people are singing in exaltation,
Another they groan like professional mourners . . .
I am appalled at these things; I do not understand their significance.

It was their desire to understand these paradoxes of life that prompted the Sumerian priests to take the relatively short step from observing the astral deities to concluding that, by their movement and the positions they took one to another, their true intentions or will could be revealed. At first the findings of the Sumerian priests would have been purely associative. They would have noticed, for example, that when a particular event occurred on earth, such as a plague or a war — or indeed something of a happier nature — it was seemingly accompanied by something happening in the sky, by a particular phase of the Moon, by the visibility of the evening 'star' or by the appearance of a comet. And if this association was later repeated, the priests naturally assumed that the two were linked.

Then, once the various cycles of the heavenly bodies had been worked out, it became possible for the Sumerians to mathematically determine when, for instance, Venus would be seen in the evening sky or, as happened later, the Moon would be eclipsed, which in turn allowed them to forecast when the terrestrial event associated with this would take place. It was at this point in time that predictive astrology began.

We can get some idea of the sort of associations that the Sumerians probably made from those that were current among the Assyrians about one and a half thousand years later. For example, here are a few that relate to Marduk (or Jupiter), Nergal (or Mars) and Ishtar (or Venus):

'When Nergal approaches Marduk, in that year the king of Akkad will die and the crops of that land will be prosperous.'

'When Marduk stands in front of Nergal there will be corn and men will be slain, or a great army will be slain.'

'When Marduk goes with Ishtar, the prayers of the land will reach the heart of the gods.'

Yet we would be wrong in thinking that astral divination in such distant times was practiced in a mass sense. What information that could be gleaned from the stars was for the king's ears only. He was, after all, both the earthly representative of the gods and the shepherd of the people, which meant that it was his responsibility to ensure that the will of the gods was obeyed and, in so doing, to obtain their blessing. And if the king knew what the gods were planning, it would enable him to use this knowledge for his people's benefit, as the Egyptian Pharaoh was able to do when he learned in a dream that seven years of plenty would be followed by seven years of famine.

In about 900 BC Sumer and Akkad were invaded by the Kuldu or Chaldeans, who made Babylon their capital city. They became strong enough to threaten the Assyrians three hundred years later, and in 612 BC they attacked and destroyed Nineveh, the Assyrian capital, thereby making themselves the masters of the Tigris and Euphrates valleys. The Chaldean empire lasted for almost three-quarters of a century, until its overthrow by the Persian king Cyrus in 539 BC.

The Chaldeans were avid star-gazers, and it was during their period of power that the astrology we know today was developed. It was they who discovered that the Sun, like the Moon and the planets, travels along the ecliptic, and they reduced the 18 member Sumerian zodiac to 12. Such celestial trimming made astrological prediction easier, while the knowledge of the course taken by the Sun enabled the Chaldeans to determine its influence on character and temperament, which is the basis of 'Sun sign' astrology. They also divided each of the 12 zodiac 'stations' or signs into 30 degrees; this allowed them to plot the positions of the Sun, the Moon and the planets with greater accuracy.

While it is true that the Chaldeans gave new names to some of the constellations in their reduced zodiac, such as the Goat (Capricorn), the Lion (Leo), and the Crab (Cancer), which are still in use today, those of the others were sometimes radically altered owing to a mistranslation of the Sumerian original. For example, the Sumerians called one of their zodiac constellations *lu.hun.ga*, which means 'hireling' or 'casual worker'. Yet when referring to it in their writings they usually abbreviated the name to *lu*. Unfortunately, the word *lu* in Sumerian also means 'ram' — hence when the Chaldeans translated the old texts, the Hireling was mistakenly called the Ram — our Aries — and by the time Ptolemy wrote his Tetrabiblos, the early astrologer's bible, in the second century AD, the name had stuck.

It was during the Persian overlordship of Mesopotamia — the so-called Achaemenian period — that personal horoscopy came into being, stemming as it did from the discovery that the placement of the Sun, the Moon and the planets in the zodiac at the moment of an individual's birth symbolized his or her appearance, character and fate. No-one is sure quite when or how this giant step took place, but it effectively meant that astrology was no longer the sole prerogative of the king or ruler. It had, in other words, become applicable to everyone.

2

THE ZODIAC SIGNS

The Ram, the Bull, the Heavenly Twins
And next the Crab, the Lion shines,
The Virgin and the Scales,
The Scorpion, Archer and Sea Goat,
The Man who held the Watering Pot
And Fishes with glittering tails.

The Zodiac Signs by Isaac Watts.

The stars in the sky are arranged in apparent groupings known as con-stellations. Most of the constellations visible in the northern hemisphere were named in ancient times, each name deriving from the shape of the constellation, which were thought to resemble either certain animals (e.g. the Great Bear), mythological creatures (e.g. Pegasus) or particular heroes and heroines (e.g. Heracles and Andromeda).

The most important constellations from an astrological point of view are the 12 that lie long the ecliptic. Because these all originally had animal names, they are collectively known as the zodiac (from the Greek *zodias*, meaning 'animal'). The zodiac constellations or signs are:

Aries	the Ram
Taurus	the Bull
Gemini	the Twins
Cancer	the Crab
Leo	the Lion
Virgo	the Virgin
Libra	the Balance
Scorpio	the Scorpion

Sagittarius	the Archer
Capricorn	the Goat
Aquarius	the Water-Carrier
Pisces	the Fishes

During the course of a year the Sun seemingly moves through each of the zodiac signs, where it remains for one month. Astrologically, the Sun enters Aries, the first zodiac sign, on 21 March, the Spring Equinox, and leaves the sign to move into Taurus on 20 April. Anyone who was born between those two dates therefore had the Sun placed 'in' Aries on his or her birthday — this being his or her 'Sun sign' — and displays those traits of character and physique that are associated with Aries. Similarly, those born at a different time of the year had the Sun positioned in one or other of the remaining zodiac signs on their birthdays. The Sun's dates of occupancy of each of the zodiac signs are given below.

The Sun passes through three zodiac signs during each season of the year:

the spring signs are Aries, Taurus and Gemini;

the summer signs are Cancer, Leo and Virgo;

the autumn signs are Libra, Scorpio and Sagittarius;

the winter signs are Capricorn, Aquarius and Pisces.

The four signs that mark the start of a season — Aries, Cancer, Libra and Capricorn — are called *Cardinal* signs; the four that lie in the middle of a season — Taurus, Leo, Scorpio and Aquarius — are called *Fixed* signs; and the four that end a season — Gemini, Virgo, Sagittarius and Pisces — are called *Mutable* signs. These seasonal positional placements reflect certain basic personality characteristics of those born then. Cardinal types, for example, are outgoing, energetic and enteprising; Fixed types are reserved, stable and conservative; and Mutable types are contrary, adaptable and somewhat unstable.

Another personality dimension is symbolized by the traditional element with which each sign is linked, these being Fire, Air, Earth and Water:

the Fire signs are Aries, Leo and Sagittarius;

the Air signs are Gemini, Libra and Aquarius;

the Earth signs are Taurus, Virgo and Capricorn;

the Water signs are Cancer, Scorpio and Pisces.

The element Fire is hot, upwardly-moving and consuming, and those who were born with the Sun in a Fire sign tend to be energetic, restless and ambitious, the type who wants to make his or her mark on the world. The element Air, which allows Fire to burn and is in turn heated and thereby moved by it, is invisible, diffuse and life-giving. Those born with the Sun in an Air sign are distinguished by their love of independence, their intelligence, and by their power to stimulate others. Hardly surprisingly, they are most compatible with Fire sign types.

The element Earth is solid, relatively immovable and heavy, and it gives to those who were born with the Sun in an Earth sign a rather dour, humourless and conservative disposition, which makes them resistant to change and variety, and antagonistic to new ideas. By contrast, Water is a fluid, cold and shapeless element, which is forever trying to run away and escape.This is why those born with the Sun in a Water sign tend to be insecure, introverted and shy, lacking both in confidence and courage. In nature, Earth gives Water support and thereby shape, while at the same time being moistened and made fruitful by it, and in a similar way Earth and Water people are mutually compatible, each gaining from the other qualities that they either lack or have difficulty in expressing, which rounds out their personalities and enlivens them.

It follows from what was said above that the most active, extroverted and pushy sign type is Aries, a Cardinal Fire sign — combining as it does Cardinal and Fire characteristics — while the most insecure, unstable and retiring sign type is Pisces, a Mutable Water sign, which unites Mutable and Water characteristics. The other sign types fall somewhere in between these two personality extremes.

ARIES
The Ram (21 March – 20 April) ♈

Aries is a small, triangular-shaped constellation, which lies, in astronomical terms, between two and three hours right ascension and 19 and 28 degrees north declination. Its brightest star, Alpha Arietis, is named Hamal, which derives from the Arabic *Al Ras al Hamal*, meaning 'the Head of the Sheep'. Hamal is a white star with a magnitude of 2.3. The two other stars that comprise the head of Aries are Beta Arietis or Sheraton (magnitude 2.9) and Gamma Arietis or Mesarthim (magnitude 4.7). The Sun was aligned with Mesarthim at the Spring Equinox in Greek times, and the star was called 'the First Point of Aries'. Delta

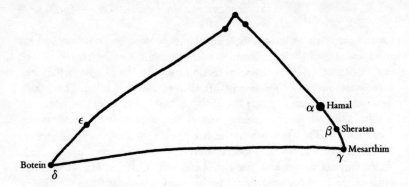

Figure 2: The Constellation of Aries, The Ram.

Arietis (magnitude 2.9) is named Botein, which means 'the Belly', despite the fact that it lies at the far end of Aries. On a clear night about 30 stars can be seen within the borders of Aries.

As has been already mentioned, Aries was called *lu.hun.ga* or 'the Hireling' by the Sumerians, and the name 'the Ram' resulted from a mistranslation of their cuneiform tablets. The Arabs referred to Aries as *Al Kabash* or 'the Tame Sheep'. In early China, Aries formed part of a large constellation named 'the White Tiger', but after the Western zodiac was introduced into that country, it was called Pih Yang or 'the White Sheep'.

The Greeks identified Aries with the golden ram that flew through the air to Colchis carrying Phrixus and Helle on its back. They said that Zeus placed the ram's image in the sky as Aries to honour its long flight. A generation later Jason and the Argonauts sailed to Colchis and returned to Greece with the ram's golden fleece.

Aries is a Cardinal Fire sign, whose planetary ruler is Mars. In myth, Mars (or Ares) was the god of war. The character of the sign is hot, positive and dry, which accords with the personality type of those born between 21 March and 20 April.

The typical Aries native is rather short in stature, yet is blessed with a strong, robust physique and a healthy constitution. The head is large, the complexion ruddy, and the eyes dark in colour, the eyebrows usually meeting above the long nose. The hair is thick, springy and plentiful — there is often a lot of body hair — and Aries men frequently sport a moustache and/or a beard. The head or face is typically marked by a scar or scars, the result of a fight or an accident. Aries women usually have small breasts. The body movements are quick, active and purposeful.

Aries people are the most egotistical of the zodiac types, which makes it difficult for them to share and to take a real interest in what others are doing. Indeed, they are prone to feeling envious or jealous of another's success or good luck, and will often denigrate what he or she has achieved.

The Arian has a lot of energy and verve, and is always ready to try something new, which is why he has been called the pioneer of the zodiac. Yet although he is a good starter, the Aries type soon loses his initial enthusiasm, especially if he encounters any obstacles. He is therefore best at starting projects that can be handed over to more patient and steadfast zodiac types, who can cope with the boring, day-to-day activities.

However, career success is important to the Arian and he will struggle hard to get to the top. But because he is impatient and restless, he often pulls the carpet out from under his own feet by leaving a job prematurely. Successful Aries people are very generous and warm-hearted, yet those who are not — that is, who judge themselves to be failures — can be bitter and self-pitying. And while an Arian can be a stimulating workmate or companion, his hot and ready temper frequently spoils his relationships.

The Aries type is direct, open and forthright, and has no use for game-playing or ambiguity. He enjoys company and likes to have a good time. His sense of humour is keen, although he does not appreciate a joke made at his expense. And his temper, though volcanic when it erupts, just as quickly subsides.

The negative Arian, however, believes that might is right. In his mad scramble after fame and fortune, the negative type is quite prepared to trample the opposition into the mud, and he is heartless and unfeeling towards those whom he considers are his rivals. The negative male Aries is a cynical seducer, who craves sexual conquest for the sense of power that it brings.

If you were born with the Sun 'in' Aries your lucky gemstones are diamonds and rubies, your lucky number is 9, your lucky day is Tuesday, your lucky metal is iron, your lucky animals are the ram, the tiger, the leopard and the wolf, and your lucky bird is the magpie.

Famous Arians include Bismark, Marlon Brando, Charlie Chaplin, Julie Christie, Doris Day, Harry Houdini, Neil Kinnock, Nikita

Krushchev, Ryan O'Neal, Simone Signoret, Peter Ustinov, Vincent van Gogh and Tennessee Williams.

TAURUS
The Bull (21 April – 21 May) ♉

Taurus is a large and impressive constellation which is centred at approximately four hours 20 minutes right ascension and 16 degrees north declination. The central triangular-shaped portion of the constellation, which constitutes the Bull's head, is formed by a group of stars known as the Hyades, the brightest of which is Alpha Tauri or Aldebaran, a first magnitude star. Aldebaran marks the right eye of Taurus. The Arabs called the Hyades *Al Mijdah*, meaning 'the Triangular Spoon'. The Taurid meteor shower originates from a point in the sky to the north of, and slight preceding, Aldebaran each 20 November. The Babylonian name for Aldebaran was *I-ku-u* or 'the Leading Star of Stars'. Beta Tauri is a double star and marks the tip of the Bull's left or northern horn. The Arabs named it *El Nath* — 'the Butting One'. The tip of the Bull's right or southern horn is formed by Zeta Tauri (magnitude 3.8). Epsilon Tauri or *Occulus Boreus* (magnitude 3.6) marks the left eye of the Bull. The Pleiades form the shoulders of Taurus; they were described as early as 2357 BC by Chinese astronomers.

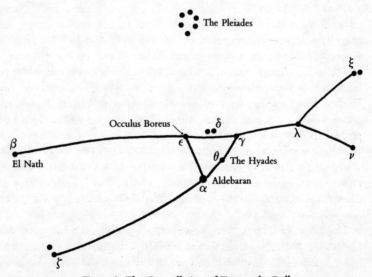

Figure 3: The Constellation of Taurus, the Bull

The Babylonians identified Taurus with the Bull of Heaven, which they believed caused storms. The Greeks, however, claimed that Taurus represented the white bull into which Zeus changed himself in order to carry off and ravish Europe, the beautiful daughter of Agenor. Europe eventually gave birth to Minos, Rhadamanthys and Sarpedon, who became the three judges of the underworld.

Taurus is a Fixed Earth sign and is ruled by the planet Venus. In myth Venus (or Aphrodite) was the goddess of love, although as we have seen she originally had a darker side, being the goddess who 'made brothers who were on good terms quarrel among themselves, and friends forget friendship'. The character of the sign is cold, negative and dry, which is reflected in the personality of those born between 21 April and 21 May.

The typical Taurean is short in stature and has a stocky physique, with broad shoulders and a thick neck. The face is open and pleasant, the complexion good, the eyes large and lustrous, and the nose straight. The hair is soft and wavy, a lock of which characteristically falls down onto the forehead. Taurus women often have large breasts. The body movements are slow and somewhat clumsy, and when walking the native has a distinct side-to-side roll.

The Taurean is the most conservative of the zodiac types and any sort of change, particularly if it is sudden and unexpected, upsets him. He is generally suspicious of new ideas, especially if they threaten to disrupt his settled routine. But while he is happiest among his family and friends, he is very sociable and enjoys a good time. He is fortunate in possessing a good singing voice and he may have musical talents.

The typical Taurus native is honest, law-abiding and respectable, yet he does have strong opinions and is not afraid of expressing them. And neither does he suffer fools gladly. He is generally cheerful and easy-going, which gains him friends, although his anger is explosive if he is pushed too far.

Taureans enjoy regular and somewhat routine work, especially that which gets them out-of-doors. They prefer to work with their hands rather than their heads, and they expect to be paid well for what they do. They take pride in what they accomplish and are generally good, steady and reliable employees.

The negative Taurus type, however, is a bully and a braggart, who likes doing as little as possible for as much as he can make. He is stubborn, difficult to deal with and set in his ways. At heart, he is the archetypal red-neck. His limited imagination and dislike of anything intellectual makes him boorish and generally condemnatory of anyone who seeks to improve himself. The negative Taurus boss, while professing love for his spouse, will hypocritically chase after the secretaries and fiddle the books.

If you were born with the Sun 'in' Taurus your lucky gemstones are the emerald, the lapis lazuli and the moss agate, your lucky number is 6, your lucky day is Friday, your lucky metal is copper, your lucky animals are the bull and the lynx, and your lucky birds are the dove, the sparrow and the swan.

Famous Taureans include Fred Astaire, Gary Cooper, Bing Crosby, Oliver Cromwell, Salvadore Dali, Queen Elizabeth II, Sigmund Freud, Adolf Hitler, Daphne du Maurier, Barbra Streisand, Denis Thatcher and Orson Welles.

GEMINI
The Twins (22 May – 21 June) ♊
The name of this constellation derives from the two bright stars, Castor and Pollux, that lie within it. Astronomically, Gemini is centred at about seven hours right ascension and 22 degrees north declination. Alpha Geminorum or Castor (magnitude 1.6) was called *Al Ras al Taum al Makaddin*, meaning 'the Head of the Foremost Twin', by the Arabs. It is actually a multiple star consisting of three binary components. Beta Geminorum or Pollux (magnitude 1.2) was named by the Arabs *Al Ras al Taum al Mu'ahhar* or 'the Head of the Hindmost Twin'. Although Pollux is presently brighter than Castor, the reverse was true in ancient times. Delta Geminorum or Al Wasat (magntude 3.8) is a double star. A meteor shower — the October Geminids — originates from a point in the sky to the north of Al Wasat in early October. Another meteor shower, the Geminids proper, originates from the northwest corner of the constellation in mid-December. The Geminids is one of the most important meteor showers and lasts for about four days.

Gemini was held to represent a pair of kids by the Babylonians, and two sprouting plants by the Egyptians. The early Arabs said that the constellation's two brightest stars were two celestial peacocks. As a human pair, Gemini was believed to represent David and Jonathan by the Jews, Romulus and Remus by the Romans, and Castor and Pollux (or Polydeuces), the Dioscuri, by the Greeks. The expression 'By Jiminy' is thought to be a corruption of the cry 'O Gemini' that was made to the Dioscuri.

Gemini is a Mutable Air sign, whose planetary ruler is Mercury. In

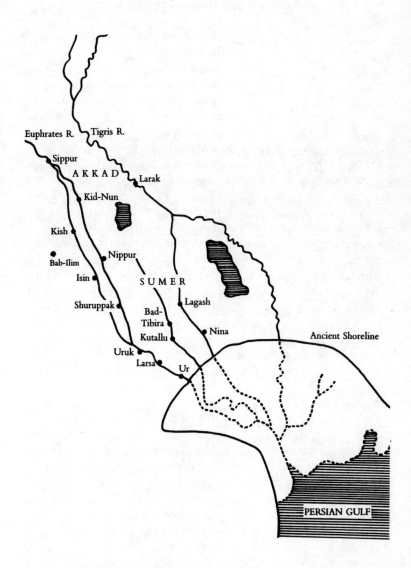

Figure 1: Sumer and Akkad

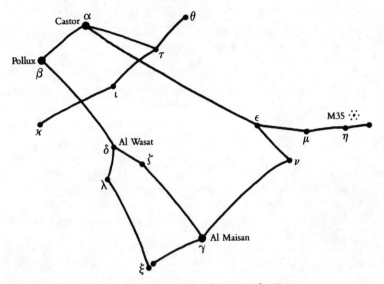

Figure 4: The Constellation of Gemini, the Twins.

myth, Mercury (or Hermes) was the divine messenger, the bringer of sleep and the conductor of the souls to the underworld. He was likewise the god of music and mathematics, theft and trickery, invention, trade and commerce, and the signing of treaties. The nature of Gemini is hot, positive and moist, qualities that are expressed in the personality of those born between 22 May and 21 June.

The typical Gemini person is of average height and has a slim youthful figure. He (or she) is often quite good-looking, the features being regular and finely-drawn. The forehead is high, the eyes bright and alert, and the hair fine and straight, although rather thin. The lips are also thin, and border a wide mouth. The complexion is good, though pale in colour. Gemini women usually have small bosoms. The movements are quick, active and somewhat impulsive.

The Gemini native has an intelligent mind and he is naturally curious. Yet his impatience and inability to concentrate effectively prevents him from mastering anything in depth, so that he tends to know a little about a lot. He loves to talk — although 'chatter' perhaps better describes his conversation — and he is a good linguist. He favours games like chess and bridge that have an intellectual content, and those sports that do not involve body contact.

Social activities are high on a Gemini's list of priorities, and he likes nothing more than to be involved with others. Yet his friendships are seldom very deep, mainly because he quickly loses interest in the other person. He also has trouble in coping with his emotions, whose demands are often repressed. This makes him emotionally cool and afraid of commitment, which is why he tends to play the field in love and to marry quite late in life. It is also the reason why Geminis often have more than one marriage.

The negative Gemini is superficial, fickle and flirtatious. He (or she) is also weak-willed and two-faced. He is quite prepared to lie and deceive in order to get what he wants, and he is adept at manipulating other people. He is noted for his hypocrisy, which is perhaps his worst feature. Natives of either sex seldom marry solely for love, and they will sooner or later cheat on their spouses. Yet because the Gemini has a weak sex drive, it is the thrill of the chase that motivates the negative type, not the actual consummation.

If you were born under Gemini your lucky gemstones are agate, opal, alexandrite and onyx, your lucky number is 5, your lucky day is Wednesday, your lucky meal is quicksilver or mercury, your lucky animals are the squirrel, the ibis, the ape and the snake, and your lucky birds are the swallow, the parrot and the linnet.

Famous Geminis include Carol Baker, Zola Budd, Peter Cushing, Miles Davis, John Dillinger, Bob Dylan, the Duke of Edinburgh, Ian Fleming, Errol Flynn, Thomas Hardy, Bob Hope, Paul McCartney, Marilyn Monroe, Priscilla Presley and Cole Porter.

CANCER
The Crab (22 June – 23 July) ♋

Cancer is an unimpressive trident-shaped constellation which is astronomically centred at approximately eight hours 25 minutes right ascension and 20 degrees north declination. It was named the Crab by the Chaldeans due to the fact that the Sun was then placed in the sign at the Summer Solstice, which marks its highest northern position, and thereafter sidled sideways from its zenith like a crab. But today, owing to the precession of the equinoxes, the Sun is placed in Gemini at the Summer Solstice. None of the stars forming the constellation are brighter than fourth magnitude, whose principal interest lies in the two open star clusters associated with it. The brightest of these, Praesepe or the Beehive, is placed between Delta Cancri and Gamma Cancri. It was once known as the Manger and the aforementioned flanking stars were

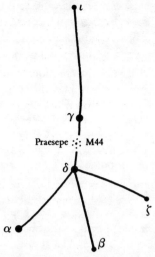

Figure 5: The Constellation of Cancer, the Crab.

called the Aselli or Asses. The second open star cluster is M67 and lies near to Alpha Cancri. Cancer reaches its midnight culmination in mid-January.

The Arabs named the constellation *Al Seratan* or 'the Crab', although one Arab astrologer, the great Al Biruni, called it *Al Liha* or 'the Soft Palate'. The ancient Chinese regarded Cancer as forming the head of a huge constellation named Choo Neaou or 'the Red Bird', which represented a quail.

The Greeks said that the constellation was placed in the sky by Hera, Zeus' wife, to honour the crab that attacked Heracles, whom she hated, when he was attempting to kill the Lernaean Hydra, his Second Labour. The crab nipped Heracles' foot, but he quickly crushed it with his club.

Cancer is a Cardinal Water sign and its planetary ruler is the Moon. In ancient times the Moon, as we have seen, was said to be male, although later (as now) it was regarded as being female. The character of Cancer is cold, negative and moist, qualities that are expressed in the personality of those born between 22 June and 23 July.

Cancer individuals tend to be rather short in stature, their lack of height being caused by the shortness of the legs. Their bodies are often well-rounded, especially in their later years, owing to the fact that their tissues accumulate water. The face is broad and pleasant, the eyes large and glistening, and the skin pale. They are sensitive to strong sunlight and find it hard to tan. They seldom have much body hair. Cancer women often have full bosoms, although their breasts lose their shape as they age. The native typically moves sideways a lot, like the creature after whom they are named.

The Cancerian is intuitive and sensitive, and is therefore easily hurt. Yet these qualities give him (or her) a natural sympathy for, and an understanding of, other people, which makes him a good friend and confidant. Both sexes cry easily, and are something of a pushover for those peddling hard luck stories. This means that they may be taken advantage of by the unscrupulous. The Cancerian is hampered by his lack of self-confidence, which makes it hard for him to push himself forward and achieve his goals. In this respect it is important that he associates himself with positive and upbeat people, who can both lift his spirits and encourage him to carry on. But because he often hides away his self-doubt and insecurity behind an abrasive and tough exterior — his protective shell — he is often misunderstood by others and thought to be a lot tougher than he is.

Both the Cancer man and the Cancer woman are happiest in their home surroundings, which are the true centre of their lives. Indeed, the Cancer woman is a natural homemaker, who loves domesticity and looking after her man. Cancer men are quite happy doing the housework and caring for the children, and if they are married to an aggressive zodiac sign type will sometimes switch roles with her, staying at home while she pursues her career.

The Cancerian is, however, quite lazy, and it takes a lot to motivate him. He likes staying up late and he also likes his sleep, which is why he finds it difficult to get up in the morning. His imagination is very rich, yet his poor practical sense makes it hard for him to translate his ideas into reality.

The negative Cancer type is emotionally and materially possessive. He (or she) hates to let go of anything, which is why Cancer marriages are often long-lasting and why, if the marriage does break down, the divorce is acrimonious. The negative Cancer is also a chronic complainer, seldom finding much right with anything. He is foul-mouthed and abusive when angered, a trait that is exacerbated by his heavy drinking and lack of self-control. Living as he does so much in the past, he is whining and self-pitying with regard to his failures in the present.

If you are a Cancer by birth your lucky gemstones are the emerald, the moonstone, the turquoise and the ruby, your lucky numbers are 2 and 7, your lucky day is Monday, your lucky metal is silver, your lucky animals are the dog, the otter and the seal, and your lucky birds are the owl and the seagull.

Famous Cancerians include Ingmar Bergman, James Cagney, Ernest Hemingway, Helen Keller, Gertrude Lawrence, Gina Lollobrigida, Dr David Owen, Rembrandt, Diana Rigg, Ringo Starr, Henry Thoreau and Andrew Wyeth.

LEO
The Lion (24 July – 23 August) ♌

Leo is one of the largest and most impressive of the zodiac constellations and bears a close resemblance to the animal it is said to represent. Astronomically, it is located beween nine hours 20 minutes and 11 hours 55 minutes right ascension and six degrees and 33 degrees north declination. The constellation's brightest star is Alpha Leonis or Regulus (magnitude 1.34), which is also called Cor Leonis or 'the Heart of the Lion'. Regulus is located at the base of a group of stars lying within Leo known as 'the Sickle'; these make up the head and shoulders of Leo. Gamma Leonis is a beautiful star forming part of the Sickle and which marks the centre-point of a bright meteor shower, the Leonids, that are seen each year in mid-November. Beta Leonis or Denebola (magnitude 2.2) lies at the far end of Leo and forms, with Theta Leonis and Delta Leonis, the Lion's haunches.

The constellation was identified with the king of beasts by the Chaldeans, although in ancient China it comprised part of a large con-

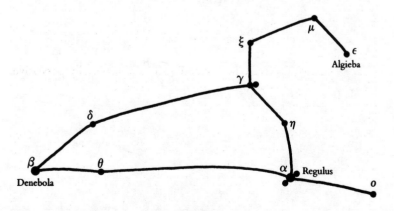

Figure 6: The Constellation of Leo, the Lion.

stellation called Choo Neaou or 'the Red Bird', which represented a quail, and was known as 'the Quail's Fire'. The early Arab zodiac was dominated by an enormous lion named Asad, which was formed from the constellations we now call Gemini, Cancer, Leo and Virgo, and from others lying adjacent to these.

The Greeks said that Leo was placed in the sky by Zeus to honour the killing of the Nemean lion by Heracles, a feat that constituted the hero's First Labour.

Leo is a Fixed Fire sign and its planetary ruler is the Sun. The Sun is, of course, a star, and while most ancient peoples regarded it as a male god, this was not true of the Scandinavians, who believed that the Sun was a girl. Leo's nature is hot, positive and dry, qualities that are expressed in the character of those born between 24 July and 23 August.

The typical Leo individual has a strong, yet not muscular or heavy, physique, and is quite tall. His upright bearing gives him a natural dignity. The head is large and often bears an impressive mass of curly and golden or light-coloured hair, his mane. The facial features are distinctly feline, the eyes and nose being large, and the lips thin. Leos tend to pick at their food like a cat and are unable to hold another's gaze for very long.

Leo people are open, energetic and enthusiastic types, who know where they are going and how they're going to get there. They speak plainly and straightforwardly, although their voices are seldom very loud. They possess a lot of self-confidence and think that they can handle most situations. They prefer to give orders and direct others, and they are never really happy unless they are running the show.

Like all those born under Fixed signs, the Leo individual is steadfast, loyal and conservative. He (or she) finds it difficult to change course once he has embarked upon a project, which may mean that he carries on flogging a dead horse, while his rivals pursue another and more pro-fitable line. He has strong opinions and is not shy in expressing them, notwithstanding the fact that this often provokes conflict with others. Yet he is one of the warmest and most generous of the zodiac types, and is always ready to help a friend in need, the poor and the down-trodden.

The native loves recognition and applause, which is why he can rarely settle for a lowly position in life. His ambition is to become eminent and respected, and the worst thing that anyone can do to a Leo is to make him look foolish. He understands the importance of education, hence he is always trying to increase his knowledge through study courses and extensive reading.

The negative Leo allows his ambition and feelings of superiority to get the better of him, which means that he can never take second place or admit that he is wrong. He is bossy and lazy, preferring to delegate responsibility while taking credit for any success that his underlings attain. The negative type loves attention and acclaim, yet is jealous of anyone else on whom the spotlight falls. At worse, he is boastful and arrogant, showy and hypocritical, supercilious and insecure.

If you were born with the Sun 'in' Leo your lucky gemstones are the topaz and the diamond, your lucky numbers are 1 and 4, your lucky day is Sunday, your lucky animals are the lion and the phoenix, and your lucky birds are the sparrowhawk, the cock and the eagle.

Famous Leos include Princess Anne, Napoleon Bonaparte, Robert Burns, Fidel Castro, Cecil B. DeMille, Eddie Fisher, Dustin Hoffman, Mick Jagger, Carl Jung, Benito Mussolini, Andy Warhol and Mae West.

VIRGO
The Virgin (24 August – 23 September) ♍
Virgo is a long and somewhat diffuse constellation, which traditionally represents a half-reclining female figure holding a stalk of wheat. Astronomically, it is centred at 13 hours right ascension and minus three degrees north declination. Its brightest star is Alpha Virginis or Spica, a double star of first magnitude that lies about 250 light years away from the Sun. It has been used as a navigational aid since ancient times. Gamma Virginis is also a double star, both of its members having a magnitude of 3.7. Two other third magnitude stars are Beta Virginis or Zavijara and Epsilon Virginis or Vindemiatrix. Numerous nebulae lie in the area of space bounded by Beta, Gamma and Epsilon Virginis. Theta Virginis is a triple star, its brightest member having a magnitude of 4.4.

Virgo was identified with the earth goddess in ancient times, although in ancient China it was called 'the Quail's Tail' and formed part of the large constellation known as Choo Neaou or 'the Red Bird'. In those days the Chinese said that the New Year began when the Full Moon was positioned to the left of Spica, which they named Keok or 'the Root of Heaven'. Following the introduction of Western astrological beliefs into China in the seventeeth century, the astrologers there called the constellation She Shang Neu, meaning the 'the Frigid

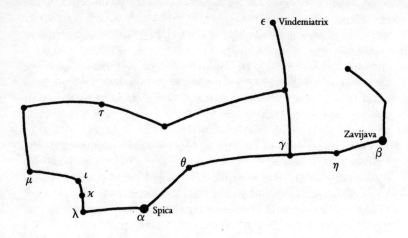

Figure 7: The Constellation of Virgo, the Virgin.

Maiden'. The Arabs referred to Virgo as *Al Adhra al Nathifah* or 'the Innocent Maiden'.

The Greeks originally identified Virgo with Demeter, the corn and vegetation goddess, but they later variously maintained that the constellation represented Pathene, the daughter of Apollo; Astaea, the goddess of justice (an association suggested by Virgo's placement next to Libra, the Balance); Iustitia, the daughter of Astraeus and Ancora; and also Erigone, the hapless daughter of Icarius, who hanged herself from a tree upon finding the murdered body of her father.

Virgo is a Mutable Earth sign and is ruled by the planet Mercury. Mercury was a very active god, who not only carried messages for the other gods, induced sleep and conducted the souls of the dead to Tartarus, but also presided over all manner of human activities like seafaring, trading and the signing of treaties. The nature of Virgo is cold, dry and passive, qualities that are expressed in the personality of those born between 24 August and 23 September.

Virgo natives are typically of average height and have, like Geminis, slim, light-boned physiques. Indeed, the delicate figures of many Virgo men give them a somewhat effeminate appearance. The arms and legs are long, the hands large — the fingers usually have prominent knuckles — and the feet small. The facial features, though moderate to small in dimension, are refined and regular. The forehead is high, reflecting the intelligence of the type, and the eyes, while large and often bright and alert in the young native, are frequently tinged with sadness in the older Virgo. The hair is dry and rather sparse. Virgo women invariably have small breasts.

Virgo people are restless and find it hard to keep still, much less relax. They hate to be kept waiting and tend to jiffle if they are. They are born worriers, their active imaginations magnifying whatever dangers or difficulties that may actually exist.

The Virgo individual is particular about his (or her) personal appearance. He hates to be dirty or to wear clothes that are grubby, unpressed or lacking in style. Such concern also extends to his living conditions, which is why the native is so often found vacuuming the carpet, dusting, washing and ironing. And although she seldom gains weight, the female Virgo is frightened of becoming fat and therefore tends to eat less than she should. Both sexes worry about their health, yet such anxiety frequently contributes to the intestional problems that are characteristic of the type.

Virgos typically have a high IQ and they place great value on education and on getting ahead in an intellectual sense. They love reading and studying, which is why they generally do well at school and college, although their natural anxiety can do them a disservice at examination time. They are good conversationalists, helped as they are by their well-read, wide-ranging minds. But like Geminis, they are scared of their emotions, which they try, as far as possible, to keep under control. They are, however, very trustworthy and have a strong sense of duty.

The negative Virgo is a carper and a complainer, the sort who always manages to find a fly in the ointment. Distrusting his emotions, he runs his life according to a strict set of rules, which he will happily attempt to force on others if he gets the chance. The negative type does not much care for sex — he is, in this respect, something of a cold fish — although some may become involved in kinky sexual practices. In fact the negative Virgo can be anti-life, being repressed and inhibited.

If you were born with the Sun 'in' Virgo your lucky gemstones are the cornelian, the sapphire, the jade and the chrysolite, your lucky number is 5, your lucky day is Wednesday, your lucky metal is quicksilver or mercury, your lucky animals are the ape, the snake and the squirrel, and your lucky birds are the swallow, the ibis, the magpie and the parrot.

Famous Virgos include Lauren Bacall, Maurice Chevalier, Queen Elizabeth I, Greta Garbo, Elia Kazan, D. H. Lawrence, Sophia Loren, Mark Phillips, Peter Sellers, Raquel Welch and Roy Wilkins.

LIBRA

The Balance (24 September – 23 October) ♎

Libra is a faint and inconspicuous constellation, the least interesting of the zodiac from an astronomical point of view. The centre of the mis-shapen rectangle that comprises its main part lies at 15 hours 15 minutes right ascension and 15 degrees south declination. Its two brightest stars, Alpha Librae and Beta Librae, were once considered to form part of the following constellation of Scorpio, the former marking the Scorpion's southern claw and the latter its northern claw. Alpha Librae or Zubenelgenubi is a white second magnitude star, while Beta Librae or Zubeneschamali (magnitude 2.6) is one of the few stars in the sky that are green, its colour accounting for the fact that Libra's planetary ruler is Venus, whose colour is green.

Libra was identified with a balance or weigh-scale in ancient times because during the second and first millennium BC, the Sun was placed in the constellation at the Autumn Equinox when the day and night length are equal or balanced. However, during the rulership of the Roman emperor Julius Caesar, his supporters, eager to flatter him, identified his image — shown holding a balance to symbolize his fairness and wisdom — with the constellation. But after his murder on the Ides

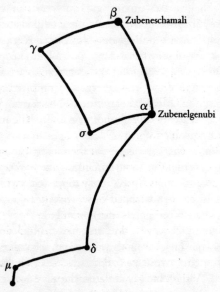

Figure 8: The Constellation of Libra, the Balance.

of March, 44 BC, his association with the constellation was forgotten, while the link with the balance was retained.

The Arabs knew Libra as *Al Zubana* or 'the Scorpion's Claws'. In ancient China, the constellations now known as Libra, Scorpio and Sagittarius together formed the Azure Dragon, which lived in the Western or Autumn sky palace. But after contact with the West was established, the Chinese named Libra Tien Ming or 'the Balance'.

Libra is a Cardinal Air sign and is ruled by the planet Venus. While we are familiar with Venus as the goddess of love, she was originally also a war goddess, these two aspects stemming from Venus' appearance in the sky as either the 'morning star' or the 'evening star', the former being favourable, the latter unfavourable, to human affairs. The nature of Libra is hot, positive and moist, qualities that are expressed in the personality of those born between 24 September and 23 October.

Libra natives are of variable height, the shortest being born close to the cusp with Virgo, the tallest close to the cusp with Scorpio. The body is generally well-proportioned, although male Librans often have one or more feminine features, such as narrow shoulders or a lack of body hair. The oval face is broad and has a good bone structure. Typically, the chin is cleft and the cheeks dimpled. The eyes are large and bright and are usually blue or hazel in colour. The hair is fine, light-coloured and, again typically, often parted down the middle. The breasts of the female native are firm and well-shaped, yet not large in size. The thick ankles are the worst physical feature.

Librans have a very good dress sense. They like to be clean and to smell nice, and they dress in smart, well-tailored, colourful clothes. When a Libran fails to pay attention to his (or her) personal hygiene or dresses in scruffy, untidy clothes, it is a sure sign that he is unhappy and undergoing problems.

The Libran character is one of the most pleasant of the zodiac types. The native is friendly, good-humoured and easy to get to know. He dislikes arguments and is always ready to go along with what others want to do. His sensible and balanced views and lack of aggression, make it easy for him to acquire friends and lovers.

The Libran, however, does not like making decisions, which stems from his ability to see both sides of an argument, and is therefore a fence-sitter. But while his friendships are easily made, they are seldom very deep. And where love relationships are concerned, he finds it very difficult to end an affair that has run its course, as he hates to hurt the other's feelings. He is fascinated by politics and he may have musical and artistic talents and interests. He also enjoys spending money, yet rarely does so rashly or impulsively.

The negative Libran is vain and selfish, spending most of his (or her) time and money on himself and his comforts. His best friend is his mirror, into which he gazes raptly. Being lazy, he dislikes exerting himself, especially if this requires him to use his brain. And while he is able to attract friends and lovers with his good looks and charm, those so lured soon realise that they are being used – the men for business reasons, the women for sex. The negative Libran is the true snake of the zodiac. He slithers around, proud of his glistening scales, yet ready to squeeze the life out of anyone.

If you were born under Libra your lucky gemstones are the opal, the chrysolite and jade, your lucky number is 6, your lucky day is Friday, your lucky metal is copper, your lucky animals are the hare, the hart and the lynx, and your lucky birds are the dove and the sparrow.

Famous Librans include Brigitte Bardot, Catherine Deneuve, Anita Ekberg, George Gershwin, Graham Greene, Rita Hayworth, Charlton Heston, John Lennon, Melina Mercouri, Rex Reed, Margaret Thatcher, Oscar Wilde and Thomas Wolfe.

SCORPIO
The Scorpion (24 October – 22 November) ♏

Scorpio (or Scorpius) is a large and impressive constellation that closely resembles the animal for which it is named. Astronomically, it is located between 16 and 18 hours right ascension and 19 and 44 degrees south declination. Its brightest star, Alpha Scorpii or Antares, meaning 'rival of Mars' is a red giant, whose baleful crimson glow is responsible for Scorpio's unpleasant reputation. Antares is also called Cor Scorpii or 'the Heart of the Scorpion'. It lies 230 light years away from the Sun and is actually a double star, one member having a magnitude of 1.2, the other of 7. Beta Scorpii is likewise a double star, its brightest member having a magnitude of 2.9. Two bright stars lie in the sting of Scorpio, one of which is called Shaula, and are known as the Cat's Eyes. There are several impressive star clusters lying within the borders of Scorpio, such as M80, which is placed between Alpha Scorpii and Beta Scorpii.

The constellation was identified with a scorpion by the Sumerians, which necessarily linked it with death and the afterlife, as they believed that the gates to the underworld were guarded by Scorpion Men. In ancient China, Scorpio, along with Libra and Sagittarius, formed part of

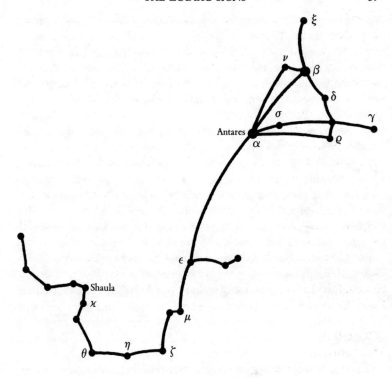

Figure 9: The Constellation of Scorpio, the Scorpion.

a large constellation called the Azure Dragon, although the Chinese later referred to it as Tien He or 'the Celestial Scorpion'.

The Greeks said that the constellation was placed in the sky by Zeus, along with that of Orion, the hunter, after Orion had been killed by a giant scorpion sent by Mother Earth, who was angered by Orion's boast that he would destroy all of the earth's wild animals.

Scorpio is a Fixed Water sign and is ruled by Mars, the red planet, probably because its brightest star, Antares, has a red hue. Mars was the Roman god of war and was said to be the lover of Venus, the goddess of love. The nature of Scorpio is cold, passive and moist, qualities that are expressed in the personality of those born between 24 October and 22 November.

The Scorpio individual is of medium height — it is rare for him or her to be very tall — and has a lithe, wiry physique. The gait is easy and relaxed, with a distinct side-to-side roll. The hands are typically held behind the back. The Scorpio face is broad and strong, and has prominent cheekbones. The long nose has a thickened tip and large nostrils. The lips are either thin and determined or full and sensuous. The complexion is either pale or has an olive colouration. The eyes are dark and deep-set; the gaze is direct and penetrating. Female natives have small breasts and are often troubled by unwanted body hair. The calves are well-shaped. The perspiration is acid.

Like the creature after whom they are named, Scorpios have a tough, resilient outer persona that hides an intuitive and somewhat sensitive inner self. But because the inner self is seldom revealed, the native is often misunderstood by others, who find him (or her) seemingly uncompromising and unrelenting. Indeed, Scorpios do have great staying power, which enables them to pursue their goals despite the difficulties that they may encounter. Hence they should never be underestimated. What success a Scorpio attains derives from his determination, his intuitive insights, and from his ability to think logically and analytically.

Scorpios thrive on personal power, which makes them demanding and rather bossy in their personal and business relationships. They never forget or forgive a wrong and will if necessary wait years to exact their revenge. They seldom have many friends, but are very loyal to those they do have.

Scorpios have a strong sex drive, yet surprisingly enough are not promiscuous. But because they find it difficult to remain detached in an intimate relationship, their sex lives tend to be intense. However, Scorpio men are not the wonderful lovers they are cracked up to be, mainly because they are too selfish.

The negative Scorpio is the most dangerous of the zodiac types. He (or she) seeks to dominate and control others by exploiting their weaknesses, taking pleasure in the discomfiture of his victims and the power he wields. He is very selfish, thinking only of himself, and he associates with others only to discover information that might later be useful to him. The negative individual has little or no concern for the feelings of others, and when crossed in any way can be cruelly sarcastic and deeply hurtful. A male Scorpio will coolly abandon a girl whom he inadvertently gets pregnant.

If Scorpio is your birth sign, your lucky gemstones are the ruby, the beryl, the cornelian and malachite, your lucky number is 9, your lucky day is Tuesday, your lucky metal is iron, your lucky animals are the wolf and the panther, and your lucky birds are the eagle and the vulture.

Famous Scorpios include Prince Charles, Indira Ghandi, Billy Graham, David Hemmings, Katherine Hepburn, Robert Kennedy, Tatum O'Neal, Stephanie Powers, Jean Shrimpton, Elkie Sommers and Jonathan Winters.

SAGITTARIUS
The Archer (23 November – 22 December) ♐

Sagittarius is a large constellation that is held to represent a centaur, a mythical creature half-man, half-horse, in the act of drawing a bow. Indeed, it is often referred to as the Centaur. It is the most southerly of the zodiac constellations, a major portion of it lying outside the zodiac band. Sagittarius is chiefly distinguished by the bright strip of the Milky Way that passes 'through' it and by the several nebulae associated with it, the most famous of which is M17, the Omega nebula. None of the stars forming Sagittarius are brighter than second magnitude, the brightest being Epsilon Sagittarii or Kaus Australis and Sigma Sagittarii or Nunki. Mu Sagittarii is an interesting quintuple star, which has an overall magnitude of 4. Lambda Sagittarii is a faint sixth magnitude star, close to which lies M8, the Lagoon nebula, and M20, the Trifid nebula.

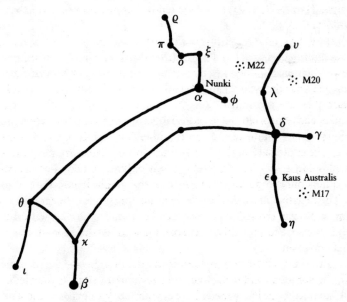

Figure 10: The Constellation of Sagittarius, the Archer.

As we have already discovered, the ancient Chinese considered Sagittarius to be part of a large constellation they called the Azure Dragon, although they later named it Jin Ma or 'the Man Horse'. It was the odd man out of the Arab zodiac, one group of stars in the constellation being called *Al Na'am al Warid* or 'the Going Ostriches' and another *Al Na'am al Sadirah* or 'the Returning Ostriches'.

The constellation was first associated with a centaur by the ancient Greeks, these strange creatures playing an important, although somewhat paradoxical, part in their mythology. For, in keeping with the double nature of their bodies, the centaurs were reknowned both for their wisdom and knowledge and also for their drunkenness and debauchery. The Greeks of Classical times claimed that Sagittarius represented the centaur Crotus, the son of Pan, the goat-footed god, and Eupheme, the nurse of the Muses, who was a skilled archer. Yet because Crotus plays such an insignificant role in Greek mythology, it is more likely that Sagittarius was originally named in honour of Cheiron, the most famous and the wisest of the centaurs, who educated several Greek heroes, such as Asclepius, Jason and Achilles. And while Cheiron was not credited with any skill in archery, he was accidentally killed by an arrow shot by Heracles.

Sagittarius is a Cardinal Fire sign, whose planetary ruler is Jupiter. In mythology, Jupiter (or Zeus) is the king of the gods; indeed, Homer called him 'the mighty Father both of god and man'. The nature of Sagittarius is hot, positive and dry, qualities that are found in the character of those who are born between 23 November and 22 December.

The typical Sagittarian native is tall and has a strong body and long limbs. His (or her) figure is slim and athletic when young, yet characteristically fills out with age, so that older Sagittarians are at best plump, at worst obese. He is blessed, however, with the most attractive thighs of the zodiac types. The face is long and the bone structure prominent, which gives it an equine look, which is enhanced by the wide nostrils, wide mouth and large teeth. In fact Sagittarians typically toss their heads like a horse. The lips are full and produce an attractive, heart-shaped smile. The eyes are usually either blue or hazel in colour. The male Sagittarian has a lot of hair in his youth, but this soon starts to drop out, hence most middle-aged natives are decidely thin on top. Female Sagittarians have lovely legs and an abundance of dark brown or chestnut-coloured hair. Their breasts are of a moderately large size, although they tend to quickly lose their shape.

The Sagittarian is essentially a hearty, outdoor type, who walks with a swing and who favours casual or sporty clothes. He is restless and changeable, and dislikes any form of restriction being placed upon him. He enjoys meeting new people and travelling, especially to exotic places.

He is a cheerful, good-humoured extrovert, who feels at his best in a group, which he enlivens with his sparkle and enthusiasm. He is fond of sports and games, particularly if these have anything to do with horses or dogs, with which he feels a natural affinity. He is honest and outspoken, having no desire to beat about the bush or deceive. Indeed, his openness can sometimes offend and may make him enemies. But while he is easygoing, he knows how to hurt when he is upset, his words flying like arrows straight to the target.

The negative Sagittarian is an irritable, selfish and rather oafish individual, whose pleasure-seeking instincts make it difficult for him to accept responsibility and whose greed prompts him to over-eat, overdrink, and fornicate relentlessly, with the result that he soon stumbles into a grave of his own making, leaving his spouse and other dependants to pick up the pieces. The negative type likes to be in charge, yet is unsuited for leadership, surrounding himself as he does with flatterers and yes-men. His warmth is reserved for those who he feels can aid him in getting ahead socially or in his career.

If you were born with the Sun 'in' Sagittarius, your lucky gemstones are the sapphire and the turquoise, your lucky number is 3, your lucky day is Thursday, your lucky metal is tin, your lucky animals are the dog, the horse and the bull, and your lucky birds are the eagle and the peacock.

Famous Sagittarians include Ludwig van Beethoven, Maria Callas, Winston Churchill, Noel Coward, Walt Disney, Jane Fonda, Uri Geller, John Osborne, Frank Sinatra, James Thurber, Mark Twain and Dionne Warwick.

CAPRICORN
The Goat (23 December – 20 January) ♑

The constellation of Capricorn has the shape of an inverted triangle, yet while it is large in size it is visually disappointing, none of its stars being brighter than third magnitude. Astronomically, it is positioned between 20 and 22 hours right ascension and 14 and 28 degrees south declination. Alpha Capricorni or Geidi is made up of at least six component stars, which together have a magnitude of 3.0. Beta Capricorni or Dabih is a double star, the largest member having an attractive orange colour and a

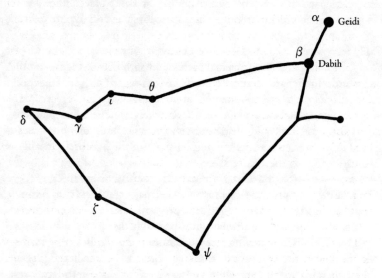

Figure 11: The Constellation of Capricorn, the Goat.

magnitude of 3.2, while its smaller, whitish partner has a magnitude of
6.2. Omicron, Pi and Rho Capricorni are also double stars.

Capricorn was identified with a goat by the Chaldeans or
Babylonians, who also named Taurus, Leo and Scorpio after the animals
we associate with them — a bull, a lion and a scorpion. In ancient
China, Capricorn, together with Aquarius and Pisces, comprised the
constellation of the Dark Warrior, although in later times the Chinese
called it Mo Ki or 'the Goat Fish'. The Arabs knew Capricorn as *Al Jady*
or 'the Goat'.

The name Capricorn is built up from two Latin words, *caper*, meaning
'a goat' and *cornu* or a 'a horn', which means that the constellation
should really be called 'the Horned Goat'. However, Capricorn is
sometimes represented as a goat with the tail of a fish, when it is referred
to as 'the Sea Goat'.

The Greeks believed that Capricorn was set in the sky by Zeus to
honour the divine goat Amaltheia, which suckled him as an infant. The
legendary Cornucopia, or horn of plenty, was reputed to be one of
Amaltheia's horns.

Capricorn is a Cardinal Earth sign and is ruled by the planet Saturn.

Saturn is linked with the sign because the Romans celebrated a festival honouring Saturn — the Saturnalia — at the time of the Winter Solstice, when the Sun is lodged in Capricorn. The nature of Capricorn is cold, passive and dry, qualities that are expressed in the personality of those born between 21 December and 19 January.

Capricorn natives are unusual in that they may belong to one or other of the two principal physical types. The first type is taller than average and strongly built, with striking, often sensual, facial features. The second type is below average height and wiry, with either a gnomeish face or one that is long, lean and serious. The smile of both types is broad and attractive, and enlivens the otherwise sombre cast of the features. The hand and feet are large, and the joints, especially the knees, are prominent. The Capricorn frame seldom carries any spare flesh and for this reason may be described as bony. Capricorn women have well-shaped, small or moderately-sized busts. The body movements are slow and somewhat clumsy.

The typical Capricorn is reserved, conservative and introverted — he (or she) is the archetypal 'thinking' person — who usually seems older than his years. But while young Capricorns are frequently precociously mature, which enables them to avoid the temptations and excesses of youth, they tend to go off the rails later in life, particularly in their 40s and 50s, when they may put their careers and marriages in jeopardy.

Capricorns dress soberly and sensibly, favouring browns and other dark colours, but often do themselves a disservice by their relaxed attitude to personal hygiene: they bathe infrequently and characteristically neglect the cleanliness of their fingernails.

Ambition is the keyword of a Capricorn's life. He wants to get ahead and do well for himself, although he is more interested in gaining honour and respect than money. He does not want or expect immediate success, but plans ahead and then works with great determination and single-mindedness to achieve his goals. Such ambition gives the Capricorn a sense of purpose, without which he would be lost and unhappy. He is careful with money, never spending it unnecessarily. Capricorn women often go into business, where they do well for themselves.

The native has a healthy sex drive, Capricorn men being the best lovers of the zodiac types.

The negative Capricorn is something of a misery. Self-obsessed and driven by a lust for power and prestige, he (or she) is preoccupied with outmanoeuvering his rivals and staying ahead of them. Cold and unfeeling, he is suspicious of the motives of those who try to get close to him, believing that they are seeking some personal advantage by so doing. The negative type is naturally reclusive, shunning both the company of others and the pleasures of life.

If you were born with the Sun 'in' Capricorn, your lucky gemstones are the garnet, the black opal and the tourmaline, your lucky number is 8, your lucky day is Saturday, your lucky metal is lead, your lucky animals are the crocodile and the elephant, and your lucky birds are the crow and the owl.

Famous Capricorns include Muhammed Ali, Humphrey Bogart, Faye Dunaway, Ava Gardner, Howard Hughes, Henry Miller, Richard Nixon, Elvis Presley, Helena Rubenstein, Maggie Smith, Mao Tse-Tung and Loretta Young.

AQUARIUS
The Water Carrier (21 January – 19 February) ♒

Aquarius is a large, yet diffuse constellation, which is held to represent a man pouring water from a large pot. Its astronomical position lies between 21 and 23.5 hours right ascension and 0 and 21 degrees south declination. The brightest star in the constellation is Beta Aquarii, which has a magnitude of 2.9. Alpha Aquarii (magnitude 3) is named Sandalmelik, which derives from the Arabic *Al Sa'd al Malik*, meaning 'the Lucky One of the King'. Sandalmelik marks the shoulders of Aquarius. During the first week of May a meteor shower, the May (or Eta) Aquarids, originates from a point in the sky close to Alpha Aquarii. The globular cluster M2 lies equidistant from Alpha Aquarii and Beta Aquarii, forming a right angle with them. M2 is about 45,000 light years from earth. Zeta Aquarii is a white double star with an overall magnitude of 4.5. Psi Aquarii is also a double star, one member having a magnitude of 4.5, the other a magnitude of 8.5.

The constellation of Aquarius, representing as it does a man pouring water into the mouth of the Southern Fish, almost certainly symbolizes the god who was believed to bring the rains that fell in the Middle East during February, the so-called 'god of the waters' or, as the Egyptians termed him, the 'Nile in the sky'. The fall of these light rains accounted for the ancients' good feelings about Aquarius. The Arabs particularly liked the sign, which is why they gave several of its stars favourable names, such as *Al Sa'd al Malik* (mentioned above) and *Al Sa'd al Su'ud* or 'the Luckiest of the Lucky'. The Arabs actually called the constellation *Al Dalw* or 'the Well Bucket'. As we have already seen, the ancient

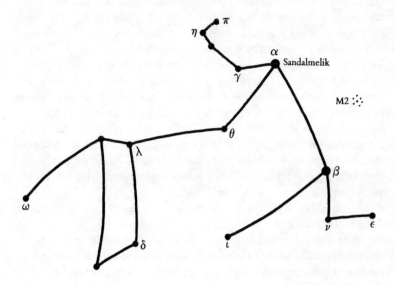

Figure 12: The Constellation of Aquarius, the Water-Carrier.

Chinese said that Aquarius formed part of a constellation they called the Dark Warrior, although they later named it Pauo Ping, which means 'the Precious Vase'.

The Greeks identified Aquarius with Ganymedes, the handsome son of Tros, who was carried up to heaven by Zeus, ostensibly to be his cup bearer, although his motive was in fact lecherous. This is made plain by the fact that the word 'catamite' is derived from Ganymedes.

Aquarius is a Fixed Air sign and is ruled by the planet Uranus. However, Uranus was only discovered in 1781, the sign having been previously placed, like Capricorn, under the rulership of Saturn, which is why Aquarians have much in common with those born under Capricorn. The nature of Aquarius is cold, passive and dry, qualities that are expressed in the personality of those born between 19 January and 18 February.

The typical Aquarius native is tall, with a lean, yet strong, physique. The shoulders are often broad and the trunk and the legs are long. The hands and feet, like those of the Capricorn individual, are large, although usually much more attractive in appearance. The forehead is high and domed, the eyebrows full and arched, and the eyes intelligent and quizzical. The fine hair characteristically generates a lot of static electricity. Aquarian women seldom have large breasts and neither are they sexy in a conventional way.

There is always something oddball about an Aquarian that makes him (or her) stand out in a crowd. His style of dress, for example, is individual, sometimes eccentric, and his manner is distant, although not unfriendly. His opinions and attitudes are different from those commonly held, often to the extent of being radical, and he is frequently involved in activities that are unusual at best, revolutionary at worst. He is, then, an individualist, preferring to 'hang loose' and 'do his own thing' rather than being one of the herd. Hence Aquarians are typically found in 'open' marriages or in freelance occupations. He or she has many acquaintances, but few real friends.

The Aquarian likes to be alone, which is why he so often shuts himself away in his room. He feels uncomfortable in groups, unless they are united by some common purpose, and so tends to avoid them. He enjoys travel, especially to out-of-the-way places, and trying new things. He often appears not really 'with it', his thoughts being focused on what might be. His ideals are somewhat Utopian, having as he does an optimistic view of human nature. He has an affinity with animals, which take to him quickly, despite the fact that he makes an indifferent owner of them. With his own kind, he makes friends most easily with either the very young or the very old.

The negative Aquarian keeps to himself, refuses to toe anybody's line, and has a disconcertingly arrogant view of his talents and abilities. He is moody, highly critical of others, and takes pleasure in ridiculing those whose ideas are different from his own. He is both unstable and changeable, dropping friends without explanation or leaving a job that had hitherto seemed entirely satisfactory to him. And the negative type's celebrated love of humanity is nothing more than an inhuman delight in launching grand schemes and manipulating others.

If you were born with the Sun 'in' Aquarius, your lucky gemstones are the amethyst, the aquamarine and the lapis lazuli, your lucky number is 4, your lucky day is Saturday, your lucky metal is uranium (but also lead), your lucky animals are the dog and the squirrel, and your lucky birds are the eagle and the cuckoo.

Famous Aquarians include Jack Benny, George Burns, Jimmy Durante, Mia Farrow, the Roman emperor Hadrian, Eartha Kitt, Norman Mailer, Wolfgang Mozart, Paul Newman, Yoko Ono, Ronald Reagan and Telly Savalas.

PISCES
The Fishes (20 February – 20 March) ♓

Pisces is a large, V-shaped constellation which lies between 23 and two hours right ascension and 0 and 30 degrees north declination, yet because none of its stars are brighter than fourth magnitude it is faint and unimpressive. It is held to represent two fish, which lie at right angles to each other connected by two cords, the Linum Boreum or north cord and the Linum Austrinum or south cord. The cords are supposedly tied together at the star Alpha Piscium, which was once known as 'the Knot of the Fishes'. This double star was named *Al Risha* by the Arabs, one member of which is pale green in colour and has a magnitude of 4.3, the other being blue and has a magnitude of 5.2. Beta Piscium (magnitude 4.5) marks the mouth of the southern fish. This accounts for its Arabic name *Fum al Samakah* or 'the Fish's Mouth'. Zeta Piscium (magnitude 5.6) is also a double star. It was given special homage by the Hindus in the sixth century AD as it then marked the Spring Equinox.

Pisces is traditionally the twelfth sign of the zodiac, although it is now in reality the first as, due to the precession of the equinoxes, the Sun now lies in Pisces at the Spring Equinox. This means that, while astrologers persist in dating the Sun's entry into the constellation on 20

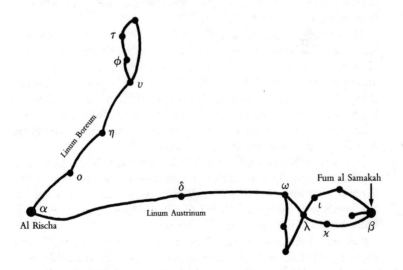

Figure 13: The Constellation of Pisces, the Fish.

February, it does not actually do so until 11 March.

With Capricorn (the Sea Goat), Aquarius (the Water-Carrier), Cetus (the Whale) and Piscis Austrinus (the Southern Fish), Pisces makes up that part of the sky which was once called 'the Great Heavenly Sea', probably because rains are more frequent in the Middle East during January, February and March, when the Sun is passing through Capricorn, Aquarius and Pisces. And Pisces is so named because late February and March was the best fishing season. The Arabs, following the Greeks, named the constellation *Al Samakatain* or 'the Fishes', while the Chinese, after the introductrion of the Western zodiac into their country, called it Schwang Fu or 'the Two Fishes'.

The Greeks accounted for the presence of two fish in the sky by means of a most interesting and unusual myth. They said that following the destruction by Zeus of the 24 earth-born giants, their mother — the Earth — slept with Tartarus and later gave birth to a dreadful monster, Typhon or Typhoeus, whose arms and legs were a mass of coiled serpents and who spat molten rocks from his ass's mouth. Typhon launched a fiery assault on Mount Olympus and the gods fled in terror, having transformed themselves into animals. Zeus became a ram, Dionysus a goat, Hera a white cow, and Aphrodite and her son Eros two fish which swam off down the Euphrates. Only one deity, the goddess Athene, retained her shape and her sense, and she shamed Zeus into resuming his normal form and standing up to Typhon. After a battle of some length and ferocity, Zeus defeated the monster and entombed him beneath Mount Etna in Sicily, from beneath which he still exhales fire to this day. To celebrate his victory, Zeus placed the image of a ram, a goat, a cow (actually a bull) and two fish in the sky. And this explains why the Romans called Pisces 'Venus et Cupido', or Venus and Cupid, these being the Latin names of Aphrodite and Eros.

Typhon apparently personifies the volcanic eruption that obliterated Thera in the Aegean shortly before 2000 BC and which caused widespread destruction in Crete and in southern Greece. Those who experienced the devastation must have thought that the gods had been frightened into impotency by the eruption.

Pisces is a Mutable Water sign and is ruled by Neptune. However, the sign's traditional ruler is Jupiter, the planet named after the king of the gods. Neptune was only discovered in 1846, since when it has been 'assigned' to Pisces. The nature of Pisces is cold, passive and moist, qualities that are expressed in the character of those born between 20 February and 20 March.

The typical Pisces native is short in stature and plump in figure. The shoulders are narrow and sloping. The short neck supports a large head bearing a lot of fine, dark hair. The eyes are large and often quite beautiful, their colour blue or blue-green. They are, however, puffy in the mornings and also after the native has been crying, which he – or, more particularly, she — does quite frequently. The cheeks are broad and full. The mouth characteristically drops open when he is surprised, which heightens his resemblance to a fish. Pisceans usually suffer from a bad case of acne during adolescence, the scars of which may mar the adult complexion. They have problems with their clothes, which never seem to fit properly, and because they somehow always manage to get soiled and creased. And likewise, their shoes tend to be scruffy and down-at-heel.

But although the physical appearance of the Pisces often leaves much to be desired, he more than makes up for it with his pleasant and unassuming personality. The Pisces-born are warm, friendly and generally cheerful people, who are both sensitive to the feelings of others and who try, whenever possible, to do their best by them. This is why they are drawn to the caring professions.

The Pisces individual is highly intuitive and tends to be guided by his feelings as much as by his intellect. He can sometimes, however, be overly sensitive and thereby deeply hurt by real or imagined slights.

He is blessed with a good imagination, which can be used creatively in the right setting. Yet in its negative expression the imagination can produce all manner of distorted and harmful images and fears. Hence it is perhaps not surprising to find that those born under Pisces have the highest incidence of mental disorder.

The negative Piscean is a weak-willed, spineless person, who finds it impossible to plan ahead or to sustain his energies. He (or she) has a low opinion of himself, yet is always ready to blame others for his faults and mistakes. The negative type drinks excessively, the alcohol boosting his confidence and soothing his fears, and may abuse drugs. He is a born worrier and procrastinator, his guiding maxim being 'Don't do today what you can do tomorrow'.

If you are a Pisces by birth your lucky gemstones are the sapphire, the bloodstone and coral, your lucky number is 3, your lucky day is Thursday, your lucky metal is tin, your lucky animals are the sheep and the ox, and your lucky birds are the swan and the stork.

Famous Pisceans include Ursula Andress, Elizabeth Browning, Michael Caine, Enrico Caruso, Frederick Chopin, George Harrison,

Victor Hugo, Edward Kennedy, Lynn Redgrave, Nina Simone and Elizabeth Taylor.

The moment in time when the Sun passes from one sign to the next, which for convenience is given as midnight, is known as the sign cusp. Those who are born during the three preceding days or the three succeeding days are known as cuspal types and are in fact Sun sign mixtures, showing some of the features of the sign in which the Sun is actually placed and some of those associated with the sign that the Sun has either just left or is about to enter. Hence if you are a cuspal type you should read the physical and character descriptions given for both signs.

But while the placement of the Sun by zodiac sign has an important bearing on the physical appearance, personality and temperament of us all, it is not the only astrological determinant of these. Of equal importance is the *rising* or *ascending* sign, which can be easily discovered if the time of birth is known . . .

3

THE ASCENDING SIGN

When I survey the bright
Celestial sphere;
So rich with jewels hung, that Night
Doth like an Ethiop bride appear:

My soul her wings doth spread
And heavenward flies,
Th' Almighty's mysteries to read
In the large volume of the skies.

From *Nox Nocti Indicat Scientam* by William Habington

As we have already noted, the Sun appears to travel around the earth along a fixed path known as the ecliptic, which takes it through the 12 zodiac signs or constellations. But while we have known since the publication of *De Revolutionibus Orbium Caelestium* by Copernicus in 1543 that it is the earth and the planets which travel around the Sun, astrology operates according to the earlier geocentric system, whose champion was the great astronomer and astrologer Claudius Ptolemeus or Ptolemy (c.90-168 AD).

The ecliptic and hence the circle of zodiac signs are inclined at an angle of 23½ degrees to the earth's equator, which means that a significant portion of the zodiac is always hidden behind the earth on any one night. However, due to the fact that the earth is rotating in an easterly direction, one zodiac sign after another appears to rise above the eastern horizon as the night progresses, each taking about two hours to do so. This rising of the signs above the eastern horizon also takes place during the day, but is rendered invisible by the brightness of the Sun.

From this it will be clear that at the moment of anyone's birth one or other of the zodiac signs will be in the process of rising above the eastern horizon, just as one will be descending below the western horizon. The former is known as the *rising* or *ascending* sign.

Furthermore, because the zodiac circle covers 360 degrees of the sky, each of the zodiac signs is considered by astrologers to occupy 30 degrees (360 ÷ 12 = 30), despite the fact that in reality they vary markedly in width. The constellation of Leo, for example, which is one of the largest, spreads itself laterally across an area of sky that is over twice as wide as that occupied by Aries, which is the smallest zodiac constellation. The point at which the horizon intersects the ascending sign, and which is expressed in degrees of that sign between 0 and 30, is called the *ascendant*. Thus if you were born with Leo rising, your ascendant could be at five degrees Leo, 12 degrees Leo, 26 degrees Leo, etc., depending on the degree to which the sign had actually risen.

When an astrologer sets up a chart, his first and most important job is to calculate the ascendant. This involves some mathematics and the use of two sets of tables, one being an ephemeris for the year of his subject's birth, the other a table of houses, which, while not a difficult procedure, is certainly daunting to the uninitiated. But fortunately, however, the rising sign itself can be identified much more simply by following the method outlined below, always providing that the time of birth is known (even if only approximately). The method does have a certain margin of error, although for most people it will be perfectly accurate.

The first thing to do is to draw the line figure shown below on a piece of paper:

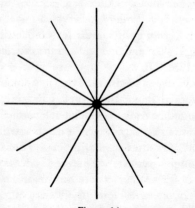

Figure 14

Next, mark in the following two-hourly time intervals:

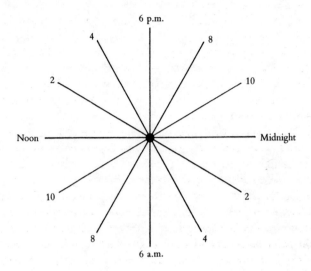

Figure 15

Then, in the segment representing the time period from 6 a.m. to 8 a.m., write the name of your Sun sign. Follow this by writing the names of the succeeding signs, in clockwise order, around the rest of the 'clock', one sign being consecutively assigned to each segment. Finally, note which sign occupies the segment where your *birth time* falls. This is your rising sign.

To make this quite clear we will take as an example a person who was born on 1 January at 11.40 p.m. His date of birth makes him a Capricorn native and we must therefore write 'Capricorn' in the segment covering the time period from 6 a.m. to 8 a.m. Then by adding the remaining zodiac signs as described above, the completed Figure 16 is obtained.

We can now see that the zodiac sign lying in the segment which represents the two-hour period during which he was born is Virgo. This man is therefore a Capricorn native with Virgo rising.

So far, so good. But unfortunately the method does not work quite so simply for everyone, due to the fact that some people were born when Summer Time was in operation, or even Double Summer Time.

In Britain, for example, everyone lives under Greenwich Mean Time

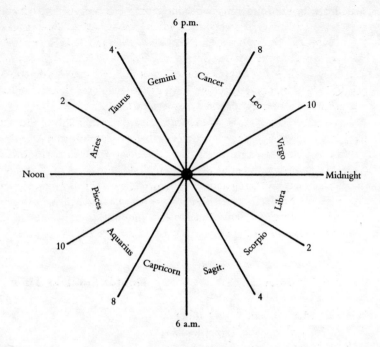

Figure 16

for part of the year — specifically during the autumn and winter — while in the spring the time is advanced by one hour, to what is known as Summer Time or Daylight Saving Time. This forward movement of the clock is reversed in the autumn, reverting to GMT, the two movements being best remembered by the phrase 'Spring forward, fall back'.

This fact is important because the method described above for discovering your rising sign is based on Greenwich Mean Time, which means that you must subtract the added hour from your birth time if your were born while Summer Time was in operation, in order to obtain your GMT hour of birth. Hence a person born at 8.30 a.m. on 14 June would actually have come into the world at 7.30 a.m. GMT.

To complicate matters, Britain was put on Summer Time continuously throughout the Second World War, except for the late spring and summer when the clocks were advanced by another hour, to give Double Summer Time, which was two hours ahead of GMT. An experimental period of continuous Summer Time was also introduced between 18 February 1968 and the end of October 1971. Thus anyone born during the War or between 18 February 1968 and 31 October 1971 will have to deduct either one or perhaps two hours from his birth time to convert it to GMT. These one and sometimes two hour subtractions also have to be made by astrologers using mathematics to determine the ascendant, although quite often they forget to do so.

It would be helpful if the clocks were advanced in the spring and put back in the autumn on the same dates each year, but unfortunately this has not been the case. However, from 1975 some standardization has taken place, the clocks being advanced by one hour at 2 a.m. GMT on the third Sunday in March and being returned to GMT at 2 a.m. ST on the fourth Sunday in October. The table below shows the dates between which British Summer Time and Double Summer Time have been in operation from when the system started in 1916, to 1974:

	Summer Time			**Double Summer Time**
1916	21 May	to	1 October	
1917	8 April	to	17 September	
1918	24 March	to	30 September	
1919	30 March	to	29 September	
1920	28 March	to	25 October	
1921	3 April	to	3 October	
1922	26 March	to	8 October	
1923	22 April	to	16 September	
1924	13 April	to	21 September	
1925	19 April	to	4 October	
1926	18 April	to	3 October	
1927	10 April	to	2 October	
1928	22 April	to	7 October	
1929	21 April	to	6 October	
1930	13 April	to	5 October	
1931	19 April	to	4 October	
1932	17 April	to	2 October	
1933	9 April	to	8 October	
1934	22 April	to	7 October	
1935	14 April	to	6 October	
1936	19 April	to	4 October	

	Summer Time			**Double Summer Time**		
1937	18 April	to	3 October			
1938	10 April	to	2 October			
1939	16 April	to	19 November			
1940	25 February	to	31 December			
1941	1 January	to	31 December	4 May	to	10 August
1942	1 January	to	31 December	5 April	to	9 August
1943	1 January	to	31 December	4 April	to	15 August
1944	1 January	to	31 December	2 April	to	17 September
1945	1 January	to	7 October	2 April	to	15 July
1946	14 April	to	6 October			
1947	16 March	to	2 November	13 April	to	10 August
1948	14 March	to	31 October			
1949	3 April	to	30 October			
1950	16 April	to	22 October			
1951	15 April	to	21 October			
1952	20 April	to	26 October			
1953	19 April	to	4 October			
1954	11 April	to	3 October			
1955	17 April	to	2 October			
1956	22 April	to	7 October			
1957	14 April	to	6 October			
1958	20 April	to	5 October			
1959	19 April	to	5 October			
1960	10 April	to	2 October			
1961	26 March	to	29 October			
1962	25 March	to	28 October			
1963	31 March	to	27 October			
1964	22 March	to	25 October			
1965	21 March	to	24 October			
1966	20 March	to	23 October			
1967	19 March	to	29 October			
1968	18 February					
1969		to				
1970				Experimental		
1971			31 October	Summer Time period		
1972	19 March	to	29 October			
1973	18 March	to	28 October			
1974	17 March	to	27 October			

Once you have made whatever time subtractions that are necessary and found your rising sign, it may be that this is the same as your Sun sign. If so, you are a double Aquarius, a double Scorpio or whatever, and your physical appearance and personality will closely match that given for your Sun sign in the previous chapter. But it will be more likely that the two are different. Should this be the case, you are advised to read both the description given for your Sun sign and that given for the sign which you now know to be your rising sign. You will notice where the latter is concerned that some of its features apply to you. Indeed, it may be that they are more strongly emphasized in your case than those associated with your Sun sign. For while we are all Sun sign and rising sign mixtures, sometimes the mix is biased more towards one than the other.

4

LONGEVITY AND HEALTH

Balnea, vina, Venus corrumpunt corpora nostra,
Sed vitam faciunt balnea, vina, Venus.

Epitaph by Martial

We all know, even though we might not like to think about it, that we are mortal, that Death stands at some point along the road we are travelling, sharpening his scythe, readying himself to lay us low. For some that fateful meeting will take place while they are still young, while for the fortunate few it does not occur until they are hoary with age and perhaps ready and willing for it to happen.

'There is no permanence,' Utnapishtim the Faraway told Gilgamesh. 'Do we build a house to stand forever, do we seal a contract to last for all time? . . . When the Annunaki, the judges, come together, and Mammetum the mother of destinies, together they decree the fates of men. Life and death they allot but the day of death they do not disclose.'

But if, as astrologers claim, the placement of the Sun, the Moon and the planets within the zodiac at the moment of an individual's birth symbolize his or her appearance, character and life pattern, do they not also foretell when that life will come to an end?

The answer to this is Yes, they do. But having said that it must be pointed out that the estimation of longevity from the birth chart is a difficult and somewhat imprecise business, which is why so few astrologers will predict when or how their clients will die. Yet there is a sound psychological reason for not doing so, particularly if the chart in question indicates a short life, because to impart such knowledge could cause worry and despondency, which might themselves contribute to the subject's early demise. And even when astrologers have predicted a long life, they have frequently been proven wrong, as they were in the case of Julius Caesar, for example.

I shall not therefore consider the estimation of longevity in detail, but will explain what can be learned about it from the Sun sign and the rising sign, which are its two most important significators.

Towards the end of the 1970s a very interesting piece of statistical research was carried out in the USA by Forest Fickling, which enabled him to determine the average life expectancy of each of the 12 zodiac types. From a variety of sources such as tombstone inscriptions, death certificates, biographies, etc., Fickling and his team obtained the dates of birth and death of some 50,000 people, half of whom were men and half women, while ensuring that an equal number of dates were gathered for those born under each zodiac sign. Using this data Fickling was able to calculate the average life expectancy of each zodiac type, with some surprising results.

'Average life spans vary widely among the zodiac sign types,' commented Fickling, 'in extreme cases by as much as 19 years. We also found that men and women born under the same signs have, with the odd exception, entirely different life spans.'

The table shows below the average lifespan obtained by Fickling for men and women born under each of the zodiac signs:

MEN		WOMEN	
Taurus	81 years	Gemini	80½ years
Aries	78 years	Capricorn	79 years
Capricorn	76½ years	Aries	77½ years
Libra	74 years	Taurus	77 years
Leo	73 years	Libra	76 years
Aquarius	70½ years	Leo	75 years
Pisces	70 years	Pisces	74½ years
Gemini	70 years	Scorpio	72½ years
Virgo	69½ years	Cancer	72½ years
Scorpio	68 years	Aquarius	71 years
Cancer	64 years	Virgo	63½ years
Sagittarius	62 years	Sagittarius	62 years

However, do remember that these life expectancy figures are averages, not absolutes. You may, therefore, live longer that the average discovered for your sign or you may not live as long.

Fickling's results confirm some long-held astrological beliefs about the longevity of the zodiac sign types, while upturning others. Capricorn natives, for example, ruled as they are by Saturn, the planet of old age, are traditionally regarded as long-lived people, and indeed Fickling found that Capricorn men live for an average of 76½ years and Capricorn women for 79 years. But Arians, however, who are ruled by Mars, the planet of recklessness and impulsiveness, are traditionally said to be fairly short-lived, due to the fact that they are more likely to be involved in fatal accidents than those born under other signs. And yet Fickling has shown that Aries men on average live for 78 years — 1½ years longer than Capricorn men — and that Aries women have an average lifespan of 77½ years. Even more surprising is the remarkable longevity of Gemini women, who are ruled by Mercury, the planet of youth, which often gives a tense, highly-strung temperament, while Virgo women, who have the same planetary ruler, only live for an average of 63½ years. Virgo women are one of the three female sign types that are outlived on average by men born under the same sign. The short lives of those born under Sagittarius accords with the nature of their planetary ruler, Jupiter, which is the planet of self-indulgence and which means that Sagittarians typically undermine their health by eating, drinking and smoking excessively.

It is unfortunate that Fickling was not able to ascertain the birth time of the subjects of his study, as this would have allowed him to investigate the influence of the rising sun on longevity. However, if we rate the 'strength' of the Sun sign in this respect by its position in the two columns above — Taurus being the strongest and Sagittarius the weakest for men, and Gemini the strongest and Sagittarius the weakest for women — then it seems likely that if the Sun sign is partnered by a 'strong' rising sign the life will be longer than average, wheras if the Sun sign is partnered by a 'weak' sign the life will be shorter than average. Thus if, for example, a Taurus man has a Cancer ascendant, then we would perhaps not expect him to live for 81 years. And similarly, if a Virgo woman has a Capricorn ascending sign then we might expect her to live for longer than 63½ years. The following examples suggest that this hypothesis is true. For instance, Karl Marx had the Sun in Taurus at his birth, which is a very strong placement, but his ascending sign was Cancer, which is 'weak'. He lived to be 65 years old. Similarly, the poet Swinburne was born with the Sun 'strong' in Aries, whereas his rising sun was the 'weak' Cancer. He died aged 71. And conversely Winston Churchill had the Sun in Sagittarius at his birth, a 'weak' placement, while his rising sun was the 'strong' Libra. He lived to be 91 years old.

The Duke of Windsor, the former King Edward VIII, likewise had the Sun in a 'weak' sign at his birth — Cancer — yet his rising sign was the 'stronger' Gemini. And he lived to be 78 years old.

The rising sign is particularly important where infant survival is concerned. It has been shown that those babies that come into the world when one of the Fire signs is rising — i.e. Aries, Leo or Sagittarius — have the best chance of surviving the experience. Babies born with Libra rising have the next best chance, while the other signs offer less protection in the following descending order: Taurus, Gemini, Virgo, Scorpio, Cancer, Capricorn, Aquarius and Pisces. Hence children born with Aries rising are much more likely to survive infancy than those born with Pisces rising.

The rising sign also indicates the manner in which we may shorten our lives. Aries rising individuals tend to lack caution, which makes them accident-prone; Taurus rising individuals, like those born with Sagittarius rising, tend to harm themselves through over-indulgence, while a Sagittarius ascendant also predisposes the individual to accidents; Gemini rising and Virgo rising natives are over-anxious, which weakens them physically and thereby predisposes them to certain ailments; those with Scorpio rising have a poor resistance to infection, which makes them particularly vulnerable to diseases contracted in old age; Capricorn rising individuals, like those with Aquarius or Pisces rising, are often sickly at birth, although they gain strength as they age; Cancer rising and Pisces rising people are prone to depression and this can cause them to undermine their health by abusing alcohol or drugs, or which may cause them to commit suicide; Libra rising individuals, like those with Gemini rising and Aquarius rising, suffer acutely from stress, which is generally weakening from a health point of view; and Leo rising individuals, who are also prone to stress-related disorders, have an inborn cardiac insufficiency that may prematurely terminate their lives.

Lastly, the rising sign is a guide to where death will occur. For example, when a Cardinal sign is rising at a person's birth, he or she is more likely to die away from his home or native land, whereas death is more likely to take place in the home environment if a Fixed sign is rising. The place of death is less certain if the rising sign if Mutable, as these have both Cardinal and Fixed qualities. However, if the Sun sign of the person concerned is Cardinal, his or her death is more likely to take place far away, while if the Sun is in a Fixed sign the reverse is true.

The zodiac signs are each identified with different parts of our bodies, which they are considered to both rule and influence. Those parts associated with the Sun sign and the rising sign are of special significance as they are more prone to disease and injury than are the others. Knowing this, it gives us the opportunity to take greater care of those parts, thereby allowing us to stay healthier.

Aries rules the head and face, which includes their various orifices and organs, with the exception of the ears. Hence if you have either the Sun in Aries or Aries as your rising sign you have a tendency to suffer from headaches and migraine attacks, head colds, eye, nose and mouth (including teeth) infections and disorders, and head injuries. Where the latter are concerned, you may already have a facial scar or scars, which has or have resulted from an old injury. Indeed, it is important that you either completely avoid those activities that carry a greater risk of head injuries, such as field sports, mountaineering, pot-holing, building site work, etc., or make sure that you wear the right safety equipment. Ear, nose and mouth infections can be minimized by staying away from crowds and infectious people, and if they are contracted you should seek prompt medical attention. You are also more likely to suffer from brain disorders and to have psychiatric problems.

Taurus rules the ears and the neck, which includes the larynx, the throat and the cervical region of the spine. This is why you are likely to suffer from sore throats, laryngitis and ear disorders if you have either the Sun in Taurus or Taurus rising. Hearing problems and speech defects are also more common, as are goitres, thyroid deficiencies, and throat growths, which may be either benign or malignant. Take note that you are susceptible to neck injuries, which means that you should avoid contact sports like rugby that commonly result in such injuries. And by driving carefully you can lessen your chances of having an accident that could result in a 'whiplash' neck injury. Make sure that you have your ears and throat regularly checked out and that you have any infections of these parts treated promptly.

Gemini is the ruler of the shoulders, arms and hands, and also of the chest and lungs. If you have the Sun in Gemini or Gemini rising you are susceptible to muscle and joint injuries of the parts in question, which can so easily result from the racket games like tennis, badminton and squash that you probably love playing. Hence you should play these games carefully so as to avoid muscle strains and joint problems. You are also prone to arthritis, especially of the hands. Should you be so affected, it is useful to remember that recent research has shown that arthritis can be alleviated by sunlight, which acts beneficially on the pituitary gland via the eyes. So spend as much time as you can outdoors. Your inherent lung weakness makes you vulnerable to chest colds, asthma, bronchitis, emphysema and, worst of all, lung cancer. You should therefore avoid working in places where you are obliged to breathe dust and noxious fumes, and you should not smoke. And because you are an anxious type, worry and stress can undermine your health.

Cancer rules the female breasts and reproductive system — that is, the vagina, uterus and fallopian tubes — as well as the stomach of both sexes. Hence if you are a female with the Sun in Cancer or Cancer rising, you are more likely to suffer from various 'female' complaints than are other women. It is important that you frequently examine your breasts for lumps and have a regular breast scan. Your naural anxiety and over-sensitivity can lead to frequent stomach disorders like indigestion, dyspepsia, vomiting and peptic ulcers, and also to menstrual difficulties. To combat these you should try to live as quietly and unhurriedly as possible, avoid unnecessary stress, and join a relaxation class. Eating a sensible diet is also helpful. And because you are prone to depression, you may find that you drink more than is good for you or use drugs like amphetamines. Do your best to limit your dependence on these psychologically debilitating substances.

Leo is the ruler of the heart and circulatory system, and also of the upper back. Should you have the Sun in Leo or Leo rising, you are susceptible to injuries of the upper back muscles and to those of the thoracic region of your spinal column. The means that you should be very careful when lifting heavy objects: always have adequate help when doing so and use the correct lifting technique. Because the heart is so important to physical health — when it stops beating, we die — you should pay careful attention to yours, for the simple reason that you are more likely to suffer from disorders like heart attacks, angina and coronary thrombosis than are those who have a different Sun sign and rising sign. You should therefore do your best to avoid stress, stop smoking, take regular exercise, and eat a balanced diet, taking care to reduce your intake of salt and those foods with a high cholesterol content. And of course make sure that you have a regular cardiac check-up. You run an increased risk of suffering from broken veins, bruising, varicose veins, and from other circulatory disorders, which can adversely affect the functioning of other body parts.

Virgo rules the abdomen and those organs found within it, notably the small and large intestine, and the nervous system. If you have the Sun in Virgo or Virgo rising you are likely to be a nervous, over-anxious sort of person, which makes it difficult to cope with stress or to sleep well. And because your insomnia may cause tiredness and irritability, you are likely to be persuaded to take sleeping pills. Your anxiety also contributes to your inherent digestive weakness, prompting the development of duodenal ulcers, a spastic colon, and other intestinal ailments. It is therefore important that you avoid stress and that you eat a well-balanced, high-fibre diet. The latter will not only benefit your general health but will help prevent appendicitis, diverticulitis, constipation and haemorrhoids, and cancer of the bowel. And by eating properly and taking regular, outdoor exercise, you will also sleep better.

Libra is the ruler of the lower or lumbar region of the back, the buttocks, the kidneys and ureters. Hence if you have the Sun in Libra or Libra rising you are susceptible to lower back muscle sprains and to slipped discs in particular, which means that you should do your best to avoid them. When lifting anything heavy always bend from the knees and not from the back, and make use of what help is available. You would also be wise to limit your involvement in contact sports or indeed in any activity that puts a strain on the lower back. You can best protect your kidneys, which are the body's filters, by only drinking alcohol in moderation and by avoiding drugs, whose toxic breakdown products are harmful to them. Your anxiety makes you more sensitive to the damaging effects of stress, which can undermine your general health. Hence try to relax as much as you can and avoid stressful situations wherever possible.

Scorpio rules the male reproductive organs, including the prostate gland, and the bladder and urethra of both sexes. If you are a man and have the Sun in Scorpio or Scorpio rising, you should be aware that you are highly susceptible to venereal infections. Thus you would be wise to avoid promiscuous sexual behaviour. You are also more likely to suffer from ruptures, prostate problems, impotence and sterility than are those born with a different Sun sign and rising sign, while both men and women of this type are are more liable to suffer from bladder disorders. It is important that you do not let the embarrassment that such conditions may cause stop you from seeking prompt medical attention.

Sagittarius governs the hips and the thighs, which are your most susceptible body parts if you have the Sun in Sagittarius or Sagittarius rising. In particular, you are likely to suffer from hip problems, such as arthritis of the hips, which can lead to a reduction of mobility and, where necessary, a hip replacement operation. It was mentioned above with reference to those having the Sun in Gemini or Gemini rising, that arthritis can be alleviated by sunlight, which brings about its beneficial effects, not by working through the skin, but through the eyes. However, it cannot do this if you wear spectacles or dark glasses outdoors, as the lenses filter out the restorative ultra-violet light. You are also susceptible to sciatica and to pulled thigh muscles. Furthermore, because you tend to eat and drink too much, you are often the victim of your own excesses. So eat more sensibly and cut down on your intake of alcohol.

Capricorn rules the knees and the skin, which of course covers the entire body surface. Hence if you have the Sun in Capricorn or Capricorn rising you are prone to knee disorders like housemaid's knee, arthritis of the knee, dislocation of the patella or kneebone, etc. Knee injuries are common in the more vigorous sports such as football and rugby, which suggests that you should limit your involvement in these or, better still, stop playing them altogether. Yet it is your skin problems that are likely to be more troublesome to you, causing as they do both discomfort and embarrassment. You are prone to such skin conditions as acne, impetigo, dandruff, eczema and shingles, as well as to those that are much more serious, like psoriasis and cancer. As many skin infections have an emotional base, it is important that you reduce your stress levels and try to live as calm a life as possible. You should also eat a healthy diet, one that includes plenty of fresh fruit and vegetables. And where skin cancer is concerned, you must avoid exposing your skin to strong sunlight, which is carcinogenic.

Aquarius is the ruler of the calves, shins and ankles, which are your most vulnerable body parts if you were born with the Sun in Aquarius or Aquarius rising. You are particularly likely to suffer from painful cramps in your calf muscles and to develop unsightly varicose veins in the lower leg. Where the latter are concerned, you may be interested to know that eating raw carrots is one of the best natural remedies for varicose veins, one or two of which should be eaten daily. You can likewise protect yourself from ankle injuries by not taking part in sports and games that require a lot of running and jumping. Make sure that you wear shoes which give good ankle support and avoid those that have high heels.

Pisces rules the feet, which explains why if you have the Sun in Pisces or Pisces rising, you are vulnerable to corns, verrucas, ingrowing toenails, hammer toes, foot ulcers, and to circulatory difficulties that may result in cold feet and chilblains. You are also prone to foot injuries. You can safeguard the health of your feet by making sure that you wear comfortable, well-fitting shoes and by paying regular visits to a chiropodist. It is particularly important that the footwear of young natives fits properly, so if your children have either a Pisces Sun sign or Pisces rising do ensure that their shoes are wide enough and long enough, and that new ones are bought frequently to acommodate their growth. Your disposition is anxious and somewhat depressive, which may encourage you to drink too much or to take drugs, or to simply not look after yourself as well as you should. In this respect you would be wise to spend as much time as you can with people who are cheerful and positive, who can get you out of yourself and uplift your mood.

5

THE MOON

Art thou pale from weariness
Of climbing heaven, and gazing on the earth,
Wandering companionless
Among the stars that have a different birth, —
And ever changing, like a joyless eye
That finds no object worth its constancy?

To The Moon by Percy Bysse Shelley

The Moon is our closest neighbour in space, a cratered and lifeless rocky sphere that orbits the Earth at a mean distance of 240 thousand miles. Its large size — it has a diameter of 2,160 miles — has suggested to some astronomers that it is not really a satellite, but rather a planet in its own right. If so, the Moon and the Earth, like Pluto and its 'satellite' Charon, constitute a double planet.

Because the Moon is large, easily visible and 'ever changing', it has always attracted a great deal of attention. We have already seen how ancient man worshipped it as a god, the Sumerians regarding it as their principal and most important deity. To the Greeks, the Moon was a goddess — Selene — although she later became closely associated with Artemis, the Virgin Huntress and the Lady of the Silver Bow. And the Romans, following Greeks, likewise made the Moon a goddess, calling her Luna.

The Moon, like the Sun and the planets, travels along the ecliptic as it moves through the sky and thereby through the 12 zodiacal constellations. Its progress through them, however, is much faster than that of the Sun and the planets, as it returns to the same point in the sky every 27 days, 7 hours and 43 minutes, a length of time known as the *sidereal month*. The *synodial month*, which is the period between one New Moon and the next, is somewhat longer, lasting as it does 29 days, 12 hours and 44 minutes. This makes up one lunation.

In Greek and Roman times astrologers placed a greater emphasis on the Moon than they did on the Sun. They believed that the Moon's position in the zodiac was the primary indicator of character and temperament, which was why Octavius had coins minted bearing the symbol of Capricorn, the zodiac sign in which the Moon was placed at this birth, when he became emperor. Present day Hindu astrologers also rate the Moon more highly than the Sun in this respect, and newspaper horoscopes in India pertain to one's Moon sign, not the Sun sign.

Modern Western astrologers, however, while not underestimating the influence of the Moon, regard it as having the strongest effect on our emotions. In a general sense it is related to the female sex, but also to the female portion of the male sex. More specifically, it symbolizes the mother, just as the Sun does the father. It also governs our intuitive abilities and our imagination. And in former times, partly because our emotions are never constant and because the Moon is associated with darkness and the night, it became linked with magic and witchcraft, and with duplicity, indecision, pliability, submission, untruth and weakness.

The Moon's dual nature reflects the two stages of growth and diminution that together make up its monthly cycle. From New Moon, when it appears as a thin sliver of light in the sky, the Moon grows in size until it becomes Full, a period of time that takes approximately 14½ days. The Moon's influence during this *waxing* or growth phase is considered to be benign. But then, from Full Moon, it diminishes in size again, until some 14½ days later it becomes New once more. This is the Moon's *waning* phase, when its influence is considered to be negative or malignant, wherein things shrivel, contract and die. Therefore in an overall sense, the waxing Moon symbolizes life and the waning Moon death. This is why those who were born when the Moon is waxing not only stand a better chance of surviving infancy, but will find that life treats them better, whereas those born during a waning Moon are not only weaker in infancy, but are more unfortunate in life, most notably with regard to those aspects of their personality that are governed by the Moon.

You can find out if you were born when the Moon was waxing or when it was waning by either consulting a calendar for the year of your birth — one, that is, that records the phases of the Moon — or an ephemeris for that year.

However, although the Moon is generally auspicious when it is waxing, the strength of its influence depends upon its position within this portion of its cycle. Indeed, the Moon's influence is somewhat weaker during the period from New Moon to First Quarter (or Half) Moon, than it is between First Quarter Moon and Full Moon. And likewise, while a waning Moon is inauspicious, it is most harmful between Full Moon and Last Quarter Moon, but less so between Last Quarter Moon and New Moon. Thus the most fortunate, where the Moon is concerned, are born between First Quarter Moon and Full Moon. Such a placement brings out the best in the so-called lunar qualities: good imagination and intuition, stable emotions, heightened sensitivity, a caring disposition, etc.

If you are able to discover the day in the Moon's cycle on which you were born, the following analysis of the effects that the Moon's influence brings about on each day of its cycle will tell you about the lunar advantages you have, and the difficulties you will face, in life.

Born on the lst day, at New Moon
You have a high energy level, a pleasant disposition, and a lot of confidence, although you tend to be too big for your boots. You are, however, sensitive and impressionable, and thus are easily disappointed and hurt. In fact, there will always be something strangely immature about you. You like trying new things, although you do not have a lot of staying power. You are particularly fond of messing about with engines and anything mechanical, which fascinate you in a rather childish way. Your luck is your best friend. You have a talent for being in the right place at the right time, which can take you far. You also have a lot of charm.

Born on the 2nd day
You are also active and enthusiastic, although your feelings can sometimes get the better of you, making you too open emotionally and hence too ready to believe a 'hard luck' story. Your excellent imagination is both a strength and a weakness, creating as it does inner scenarios that may be mistaken for reality. This sometimes leads you to distort the truth, which may have others branding you as a liar. Yet because you are generally lucky, you should go further in life than your talents might otherwise suggest.

Born on the 3rd day
You have a rising spirit and a pleasant and engaging personality, which attracts people to you and thus brings you a lot of friends. Indeed, you

enjoy socializing and getting out and about. Your strong moral sense makes you both trustworthy and dependable, and prompts you to feel protective towards the poor and the unfortunate, which inclines you to charitable work, helping the handicapped and the aged, etc. You have a good intuition and this helps you to make the right decisions. You are lucky in being able to make friends with influential people, who will, in turn, help you to get ahead.

Born on the 4th day
You are unusual in that while you give others the impression of being confident and self-contained, you actually have a lot of doubts about yourself and your abilities, which makes you somewhat fearful of the world and of the future. Yet despite this, you hate being tied down and restrained, and hence will eventually leave a job or a situation that hampers your freedom of choice or movement. And like those mentioned above, you are generally fortunate in what you do, although you will suffer certain unexpected reverses.

Born on the 5th day
Like those born at New Moon, you are hopeful and energetic, which are positive traits, but are also rather proud of yourself and your accomplishments, which are not. Indeed, you can turn others against you by your vocal style of self-advertising, which can hinder your forward progress. Yet your native intelligence and persuasive tongue gives you a head start in any career that involves selling, public relations or promotion, etc. However, you are both changeable and contrary, and you have difficulty in making up your mind. Hence you may fail to take advantage of those opportunities that come your way.

Born on the 6th day
You have an engaging manner and a friendly disposition, although you are rather shy and unsure of yourself. You like to look nice and thus tend to spend quite a lot of your money on your clothes and on your appearance generally. This self-attention helps to bolster your confidence and improve your mood. You are essentially a homebody and your family occupies a place of central importance in your life. You will always gain most from your personal relationships, while those involving work or business colleagues will be less successful. This means that you should not expect to reach the top rung of any job or profession that you enter.

Born on the 7th day

You probably had a rather difficult childhood and youth, which is why you are not as emotionally stable or as self-confident as you would like to be. And yet you are quite creative and imaginative, talents that can, with the right help, take you far. Your dress sense, however, leaves something to be desired, thus you seldom look as smart as you would like to. You enjoy learning and finding things out, characteristics that, with your warm and sympathetic nature, make you a natural educator.

Born on the 8th day, at First Quarter Moon

Your disposition is serious and thoughtful, which makes it difficult for you to laugh and enjoy a joke. Yet you are quietly confident and ambitious, and you are able to work hard to achieve what you want in life. You are particularly well-suited for a career in business or the professions, where your caution and steadfastness can help you advance yourself. Because you feel rather uncomfortable in your relationships with the opposite sex, you may not marry until quite late in life. You dislike change and anything that creates disorder and uncertainty.

Born on the 9th day

You are a positive and outgoing type of person: you speak your mind, enjoy social activities, and like to start anything new straight away. Yet while you have a lot of energy and enthusiasm, you lack staying power and become easily discouraged when things don't immediately plan out as you had hoped. Coping with details both bores and irritates you, hence you function best as an initiator. Your forward movement in life will always consist of a series of stops and starts, although it will seldom, if ever, be regressive.

Born on the 10th day

You are fortunate in having an outgoing, optimistic personality, which is helped by a good intuitive sense of what you should do next. You like tackling new challenges, and nothing gives you greater pleasure than solving a seemingly insoluble problem. Because you enjoy travelling you may well go abroad to work or live, if only temporarily. Should the other planets be favourably placed in your birth chart, you will do well for yourself financially, perhaps to the extent of becoming quite wealthy.

Born on the 11th day

While you are lively and outgoing, you are blessed with a subtle understanding of human nature, which makes it easy for you to gain friends and to impress those who can help you. Yet you suffer, however, from intermittent periods of depression, and these can have you questioning the value of what you are doing. Your natural sympathy for others attracts you to those jobs that involve helping and caring, such as nursing, social work, etc. Indeed, in such a field you can rise quite high and earn much respect.

Born on the 12th day

Although you have a somewhat hearty personality, which will encourage you to get out and have fun while you are young, you are basically very moral in your beliefs and aspirations. In fact you sense that there is a dimension of the spirit, which both sustains you and gives you comfort. You enjoy being outdoors and you are a keen sportsman. Yet because you lack ambition in a worldly sense and are not very hardworking, you probably won't climb right to the top of your employment ladder.

Born on the 13th day

You like having order and certainty in your life and when you have them you are quite capable of working hard and achieving your ambitions. You are fortunate in generally gaining the help of those who matter, who can both instruct and advise you. Yet you find it difficult to cope when upsets occur or when your plans encounter an unexpected obstacle. You love working with your hands, especially in a creative way, which attracts you to such activities as pottery, sculpture, dress design, painting, etc. You tend, however, to be moody, and when you are you become very uncommunicative, which puzzles others.

Born on the 14th day

You are pleasant, quiet and generous, the type who gets on well with others and who is well liked. You dislike injustice, hence you are always ready to speak up for and help those who are being treated unfairly. You get on well with the opposite sex and, if you are not yet married, you will be looking forward to the day that you are. You have ambitions for yourself, although unforeseen difficulties are always springing up to hinder your forward progress. You find it hard to save money, mainly because you have a weakness for gambling.

Born on the 15th day, at Full Moon
You have a strong and somewhat overbearing personality, which can make you very intimidating. Indeed, you like to get your own way. Yet your bluster is a cover for your inner uncertainty, as you are by no means always sure that what you do is right. Ideally, you want to reach a high position in life, so that people look up to you and give you respect. Yet although this is your goal, your contrary nature too often has you changing direction just when the olive branch is within your reach.

Born on the 16th day
You are ambitious and want to get ahead, but your forward movement in the fields you find most attractive, i.e. fashion, entertainment, art and design, etc., is hampered by your love of money and by your serious and rather inflexible disposition. This may mean that you will opt for a steady job or enter one of the professions, which could lead to you regretting not having been more adventurous as you get older. You are industrious and determined, although you dislike being told what to do. This can prompt sudden changes of job if you feel put upon and may stop you from achieving your goals.

Born on the 17th day
Your slow metabolism makes it hard for you to stay slim, hence you and food will always have something of a running battle. However, you are kind and considerate, which gains you friends, although your natural despondency can on occasions make you difficult to be with. Your interests are centred on your home and family, but you would also like to have a career that allows you to express your artistic talent. But if you do work and run a home, you will find that the demands of the one too often interfere with those of the other, thereby making it difficult for you to achieve the success you would like in either.

Born on the 18th day
You know, or at least you think you know, what you want out of life and you are very determined and pushy in realizing your ambitions. Yet your quick temper and high-handed manner creates problems for you with your associates, which loses you their support and encouragement. Your problems with others are compounded by your inability to think your ideas through and to plan ahead properly. You dislike dealing with details and are irritated by those who question your methods. And while you are good at making money, you have difficulty in keeping it. You are also hypocritical.

Born on the 19th day

You are a very bright and breezy type of person, full of energy and enthusiasm. This can be stimulating and rather charming when you are young, but becomes somewhat unnerving and irritating to others as you age. For you will never properly mature, which may have you behaving inappropriately and perhaps foolishly in your middle years. However, you have a sharp temper when crossed and you say what you think. You are particularly suited for any job that involves selling or promoting, and you are a good public speaker. You like to be in charge, yet you are not wholly suited to such a role.

Born on the 20th day

You have a good imagination and a lot of creative potential, yet you are held back by your lack of confidence and by your inability to focus your mind. You are constantly pulled this way and that by the ideas and suggestions of others, which makes it hard for you to decide what is right and how to proceed. Such indecision will hinder you in achieving your goals. Yet your intuitive understanding of the problems of others makes you an excellent counsellor and confidant. Ideally, you need to find someone who can direct your energies and stop you from wasting your talents.

Born on the 21st day

Despite your occasional periods of self-doubt and uncertainty, you are basically a happy, outgoing and cheerful soul. You like to laugh and have a good time, and you are always ready to listen to the problems of those you are with. In fact your general sensitivity and good sense make you well-suited to those professions like social work, psychiatry and medicine, that deal with personal problems. You are quite religious and may even be an active member of the church. You tend, however, to be too self-critical and to blame yourself for the mistakes made by your family and friends. This causes you inner disquiet and some unhappiness.

Born on the 22nd day, at Last Quarter Moon

You are essentially a quiet, home-loving type, who feels most comfortable and relaxed in the company of your family and close friends. Yet despite this, you unfortunately have quite strong worldly ambitions, although you lack the necessary drive and resolve to achieve them. Hence you may feel unfulfilled and frustrated. You are also very sensitive to criticism and can be deeply hurt by even innocuous remarks if they are misconstrued. Yet you are kind and forgiving, and are generally well-liked.

Born on the 23rd day
You like travel and change, and the lure of foreign parts exerts a strong attraction for you. In fact you will change your job and your place of residence more than most, and you may even go abroad to live. However, you will never feel entirely happy about making such moves as they will separate you from your roots, which are important to you, and cause upset in the lives of others. In fact you will sometimes feel quite guilty about them. You have a well-developed spiritual sense and a love of people, which makes you ideally suited, in many respects, for relief work and missionary work.

Born on the 24th day
Although you are shy and rather uncertain of yourself, you have a kind heart and a pleasant, engaging manner, which attracts others to you. You are close to your family, who will always be very important to you. Yet you can, however, be very stubborn once you have made up your mind and this can lead to unnecessary rows with those you love the most. You also tend to rely too much on your intuitive impressions which, while good, are not always accurate. Hence you quite often make mistakes.

Born on the 25th day
You are unusual in that while you are rather shy and withdrawn, preferring to follow the pack instead of leading it, you have an enquiring mind, a love of travel and adventure, and a short temper. These contrasting characteristics make it hard for you to find the right balance in your life, which in turn makes you feel unhappy. Ideally, therefore, you need the support of someone, such as a spouse, who can help direct you and give you encouragement when things go wrong. You will gain most success in a field that allows you to express your quite considerable artistic talents.

Born on the 26th day
You are a quiet, reserved sort of person to whom a secure, loving family life will always be of great importance. You were devoted to your parents as a child and you will certainly look after them when they get old. Your happiness in life largely depends upon your choice of

marriage partner. If you are lucky in this respect you will grow and bloom, but if not you will feel desolate and miserable. You love children and will want one or more of your own, although you won't stand any nonsense from them. You set high standards for yourself and have a strong notion of right and wrong.

Born on the 27th day

You are very moody and unpredictable, some days feeling bright and happy, but on others quite the reverse. Indeed, if there are negative influences in your birth chart, you may at worst be manic-depressive. You have a ready temper when upset and you tend to see things in black-and-white terms, which makes it difficult for you to interact with those who have different views. Hence you will find it hard to make progress in a career and you must expect to have a lot of disagreements with your colleagues. And yet, ironically, your natural sensitivity and concern for others can, in the right situations, make you an excellent adviser and solver of problems.

Born on the 28th day

Although you are also somewhat emotional and unpredictable, you have ambitions for yourself and you like to be noticed. But you are not a particularly sociable type, hence you find it difficult to make friends. You have a good financial sense and you know the value of money, thus you tend to be careful with how you spend it. You need to have a settled and stable home situation, but also sufficient freedom to indulge yourself occasionally. You judge others rather harshly and expect higher standards of them than you do of yourself.

Born on the 29th day

You are a secretive, discreet sort of person, particularly where your emotions are concerned, which makes it hard for others to really get to know and understand you. This gives you a certain aura of mystery, which you rather enjoy. You like being on your own and your hobbies and interests tend to be those that you can do by yourself. You have a clever and astute mind, which can take you far, although you would prefer to work behind the scenes. Indeed, you shun the limelight whenever possible, even though you will often deserve to be in it. Your best friends are those you grew up with, to whom you will always be very loyal. Although you are basically quite honest, you will when necessary use underhand methods to get what you want.

However, while the Moon's angular relationship to the Sun at our birth symbolizes the emotional component of our personality and, although to a lesser extent, our fate, it continues to influence us, like the Sun and the planets, throughout our lives — affecting our mood and, in turn, our behaviour. It also alters our physical functioning, particularly that of the reproductive system.

It has long been known that the Full Moon has a predominantly negative effect on us, a fact that was scientifically verified by Dr Leonard J. Ravitz of Duke University in 1962. His research showed that the electrical activity of the brain is disturbed at Full Moon, which resulted in more excitable, unpredictable and aggressive behaviour. This disturbance is most pronounced in those who are mentally ill and is the reason why such people were once called 'lunatics'.

And indeed, police records in both Britain and America show that at Full Moon there is a general increase in anti-social behaviour among the population at large. There is, for example, more drunkenness and disorderly conduct, and more arson attacks, assaults, rapes, riots and murders. Such an increase also takes place at New Moon, although it is less marked.

There are also more suicides among both men and women at Full Moon. However, women are especially likely to commit violence against themselves and to attempt suicide then.

The reason why human behaviour is negatively influenced by the Full Moon, and to a lesser extent by the New Moon, is still unclear, but it may be brought about by the change that occurs in the ionic composition of the atmosphere at such times. At both New Moon and Full Moon the ionic blance of the atmosphere shifts in favour of positive ions, which are known to adversely affect our mood, making us more anxious and irritable. Negative ions, on the other hand, produce more buoyant and alert feelings, and therefore have a positive effect on us.

The increase in the number of positive ions in the atmosphere at New Moon and Full Moon may also account for the fact, reported in a 1977 Russian study, that epileptics are 1.5 times more likely to suffer from a seizure then.

Perhaps more puzzling is the discovery by Dr Edson Andrew in the 1950s that 82 per cent of his patients' bleeding crises took place between First Quarter Moon and Last Quarter Moon, with a peak at Full Moon. This led Dr Norman Shealy to later recommend that 'surgeons should definitely not perform any surgery except emergencies during Full Moon.'

It is well-known that the reproductive cycles of many sea creatures are timed by the Moon. The Californian cuttlefish, for example, always spawns three days after a Full Moon, while the mating swans of the South Sea Palolo worm take place at Last Quarter Moon in October and November.

The 28-day human female menstrual cycle suggests a similar linkage between the Moon and ourselves. Indeed, it was Charles Darwin himself who once commented: 'Man is descended from fish; why should not the 28-day feminine cycle be a vestige of the past when life depended on the tides, and therefore the Moon?'

It now seems probable that women once menstruated at New Moon and ovulated at Full Moon. If so, ovulation would have been triggered by the increased illumination at Full Moon, which would have been complemented by the greater amount of sexual activity then, the two together making pregnancy more likely.

This phasing of menstruation and ovulation with the New Moon and the Full Moon has now largely been lost, at least in the civilized world, due to the widespread use of electric lighting.

However, the Moon is still very important in another respect, as it plays a significant role in determining the sex of a child.

This remarkable finding was made by Dr Eugen Jonas at the Bratislava Clinic of Gynaecology in the 1960s. He showed that if conception occurs when the Moon is placed in one of the positive or male signs of the zodiac — that is, Aries, Gemini, Leo, Libra, Sagittarius or Aquarius — the child will be a boy, while if it happens when the Moon is in a negative or female sign — i.e. Taurus, Cancer, Virgo, Scorpio, Capricorn or Pisces — the child will be a girl. Some 8,000 women took part in the test trial that Jonas arranged and the effect was found to be 95 per cent accurate. This gives every woman the means of choosing the sex of her children, by simply restricting intercourse to those days when the Moon occupies a sign that has the same 'gender' as she would wish for her child. All she had to do is to buy an ephemeris for the year in question, which will tell her the dates when the Moon enters each sign of the zodiac (Note: the Moon remains in each sign for about 2¼ days).

The Moon does not, of course, determine the sex of a child by itself. An ovum or egg develops into a boy or a girl depending on the type of spermatozoon that has fertilized it. The sperms come in two genetical types, X and Y, whereas the eggs are all X. If an X sperm penetrates the egg, the result is an XX embryo, which develops into a girl; whereas if the egg is fertilized by a Y sperm, the result is an XY embryo, which develops into a boy. Because the two types of sperm are produced in approximately equal numbers, which gives both a 50-50 chance of reaching the egg, the Moon must in some way be able to tip the balance in favour of one at the expense of the other.

But how does it do this? Unfortunately, nobody really knows the answer to this question. However, it is known that sperm is sensitive to a weak electrical charge, which has the effect of separating the two types. Hence if the Moon can alter the electrical organization of the womb, this may at one point — i.e. when the Moon is lodged in a male sign — retard the movement of X sperm in favour of Y sperm, and vice versa. The Moon certainly causes changes in the Earth's magnetic field, and in so doing it could thereby influence the environmental conditions within the female reproductive tract.

Jonas also discovered that a woman is most fertile when the angle between the Moon and the Sun is the same as it was at the time of her birth. Thus a woman born at New Moon will be most fertile then, always providing that the New Moon occurs at the time in her menstrual cycle when she is ovulating.

And perhaps more enigmatically, Jonas likewise found that if a woman is born at Full Moon she is more likely to miscarry or give birth to a retarded child if the child was conceived at Full Moon. Hence women born at Full Moon should certainly avoid becoming pregnant when the Moon is full.

6

THE PLANETS
AND FUTURE TRENDS

This was the man who once was free
To climb the sky with zeal devout
To contemplate the crimson sun,
The frozen fairness of the moon —
Astronomer once used in joy
To comprehend and to commune
With planets on their wandering ways.

From *The Consolation of Philosophy* by Boethius

The Solar System consists of a medium-sized star, the Sun, around which orbit nine planets and their attendant satellites, tens of thousands of rock fragments or asteroids, dozens of comets and large quantities of dust.

The earth-bound astrologer, however, refers to both the Sun and the Moon as planets, which adds them to the list of real planets — Mercury, Venus, Mars, Jupiter, Saturn, Uranus, Neptune and Pluto — that are considered to have an influence on us. Indeed, it is the placement of the planets in the zodiac at the moment of our birth that symbolizes our physical type, our character and talents, and our fate.

Yet the planets' influence on us does not stop at our birth, but continues throughout our lives. And this is why we can, through a knowledge of their future positions, determine those periods which will be good for us and those which will be less kind. Such foreknowledge can thereby allow us to take advantage of the former and take extra care during the latter, so enabling us to get the best out of life.

Two planets are of special importance in this respect, the first being that which rules our Sun sign and the other the one that rules our rising sign. For it is their position in the zodiac that provides the key to determining which periods in the years ahead will be favourable and which unfavourable.

As we have already noted, each planet rules a particular sign or signs: The Sun rules Leo; the Moon, Cancer; Mercury, Gemini and Virgo; Venus, Taurus and Libra; Mars, Aries and Scorpio; Jupiter, Sagittarius and Pisces; and Saturn, Capricorn and Aquarius. However, since the discovery of the 'new' planets Uranus, Neptune and Pluto, it has become fashionable to ascribe the rulership of Aquarius to Uranus, Pisces to Neptune, and Scorpio to Pluto. Yet because these planets are so distant and slow moving, those born under Aquarius, Pisces and Scorpio, or who have one of these signs ascending at their birth, will find it more satisfactory to take guidance from the placement of their traditional planetary ruler. Hence if, for example, your Sun sign is Aquarius and your rising sign is Pisces, then your two planetary rulers are Saturn and Jupiter, although in modern terms they are Uranus and Neptune. But while most people have two planetary rulers, due to the fact that they have a different Sun sign and rising sign, some will only have one, as the Sun was placed in their rising sign at their birth. Such people are referred to as a 'double Aries', a 'double Gemini', or whatever.

When a planet is passing through the zodiac sign that it rules it is said to be 'strong' or 'favourable'. But there is one placement that is better than this, and that is when the planet passes through the zodiac sign wherein it is exalted. The influence of a planet in exaltation is very favourable for those with whom it is linked — that is, by being the ruler of their Sun sign or rising sign — and the period of time it spends there will be most fortunate. The worst period, on the other hand, occurs when a planetary ruler is moving through the zodiac sign wherein it is debilitated, when its influence is either severely weakened or malignly directed. Such a period of time throws up all manner of frustrations, difficulties and disappointments, which makes it very negative in tone.

The table below shows the zodiac signs in which each of the traditional planets is either exalted or debilitated:

Planet	Exalted in	Debilitated in
Sun	Aries	Libra
Moon	Taurus	Scorpio
Mercury	Virgo	Pisces
Venus	Pisces	Virgo

Planet	Exalted in	Debilitated in
Mars	Capricorn	Pisces
Jupiter	Cancer	Capricorn
Saturn	Libra	Aries

In general, therefore, when one or other of your planetary rulers is passing through a sign that it rules, wherein it is said to be strong, it favours those qualities of character, health aspects, directions, activities and occupations that are associated with the planet. They are also, although more positively, favoured when the planet is exalted. A planet in exaltation also brings about improved relationships with others, most notably with children and older people, and makes it easier for you to achieve your ambitions. Conversely, when one or other of your planetary rulers is debilitated, you will find that certain of your personal relationships are adversely affected (the chief of which are those with your parents and other family members), that you may experience losses of one sort or another, and that difficulties arise in your job or career which hinder your forward progress.

We shall consider the placement of the Sun, Mercury, Venus, Mars, Jupiter and Saturn in the signs that they rule, and in those where they are exalted and debilitated, over a period of five years. The best periods for you are those when one, or perhaps both, of your planetary rulers are exalted, while the worst periods occur when one, or again perhaps both, is debilitated.

Lack of space prevents this being done for the Moon, which is the fastest traveller through the zodiac. Should one of your planetary rulers be the Moon, you are advised to buy either an almanac or an ephemeris for the time period in question, which will give you its future zodiac positions. But you are specifically favoured when the Moon is waxing, when things will be somewhat easier for you. A good calendar or diary will show the phases of the Moon.

The Sun
The Sun is strong in Leo, which it rules, exalted in Aries, and debilitated in Libra. A well-placed Sun fosters overall good health, although it particularly favours that of the heart, arterial system and the right eye. It likewise improves vigour and confidence, increases influence and prestige, brings about a promotion or some special honour, gains the attentions of those in authority, and benefits any dealings involving gold.

Such a placement also positively influences one's relationship with one's father, travel in an easterly direction, and visits to royal palaces, castles, forts, wooded or mountainous country, etc.

Because the Sun travels through the zodiac in one year, it spends one month in each of the signs. This means that it will always be placed in Leo, Aries and Libra between approximately the same dates every year.

Sun in Leo:

23 July 1989	to	23 August 1989
24 July 1990	to	23 August 1990
24 July 1991	to	23 August 1991
23 July 1992	to	23 August 1992
23 July 1993	to	23 August 1993

Sun exalted in Aries:

21 March 1989	to	20 April 1989
21 March 1990	to	20 April 1990
22 March 1991	to	20 April 1991
21 March 1992	to	19 April 1992
21 March 1993	to	20 April 1993

Sun debilitated in Libra:

23 September 1988	to	23 October 1988
24 September 1989	to	23 October 1989
24 September 1990	to	23 October 1990
24 September 1991	to	23 October 1991
23 September 1992	to	23 October 1992

The Moon

The Moon is strong in Cancer, which it rules, exalted in Taurus, and debilitated in Scorpio. When the Moon is well-placed it emotionally calms and generally improves the spirits of those whose ruler it is. It also benefits the digestion, alleviates ailments of the female reproductive tract, and gives better sleep. Similarly, it also stimulates the imagination and thereby one's creativity, increases psychic receptivity, and improves work and career conditions and opportunities, particularly for those working in a lunar occupation, such as writing, nursing, psychiatry, bartending, waitressing, etc. It may also bring wealth and a measure of fame. Relations with one's mother and with young children are improved, and travel is made easier and more pleasant, especially that taken by boat or in a north-westerly direction.

Mercury

Mercury is strong in Gemini, which it rules, exalted in Virgo, which it also rules, and debilitated in Pisces. When Mercury is well-placed it favours the health of the nervous system and of the lungs and chest, improves friendships and makes new friendships more likely, gives greater fluency and persuasiveness, benefits study and the passing of examinations, and brings advances in any field or career linked with it, such as writing and publishing, acting and drama, dancing, public relations, mediation, trade, politics, etc. It also favours relations with one's maternal uncles, travel in a northerly direction, and the study of astrology and other esoteric pursuits.

Mercury in Gemini:

30 April 1989	to	28 May 1989
13 June 1989	to	6 July 1989
13 June 1990	to	27 June 1990
6 June 1991	to	19 June 1991
27 May 1992	to	9 June 1992
19 May 1993	to	2 June 1993

Mercury exalted in Virgo:

6 August 1989	to	26 August 1989
27 September 1989	to	11 October 1989
30 July 1990	to	5 October 1990
27 July 1991	to	19 August 1991
11 September 1991	to	28 September 1991
4 September 1992	to	19 September 1992
27 August 1993	to	11 September 1993

Mercury debilitated in Pisces:

11 March 1989	to	28 March 1989
4 March 1990	to	19 March 1990
25 February 1991	to	11 March 1991
17 February 1992	to	3 March 1992

4 April 1992	to	14 April 1992
8 February 1993	to	15 April 1993

Venus

The planet Venus is strong in Taurus and Libra, which it rules, exalted in Pisces, and debilitated in Virgo. A well-placed Venus beautifies the appearance and enhances the health of the throat, ears, abdominal organs and nervous system. It similarly stimulates the love life (it may even bring about a marriage), heightens marital harmony, benefits relations with one's children, and helps those engaged in artistic pursuits to advance themselves. It also benefits those who buy or sell clothes, perfumes, ornaments, jewellery, flowers, and other Venus-ruled products. It favours travel in a south-easterly direction and visits to the theatre and to restaurants.

Venus in Taurus:

17 April 1989	to	11 May 1989
30 May 1990	to	25 June 1990
19 March 1991	to	13 April 1991
2 May 1992	to	26 May 1992

Venus in Libra:

30 October 1988	to	23 November 1988
19 August 1989	to	12 September 1989
6 October 1990	to	23 October 1990
10 November 1991	to	6 December 1991
1 September 1992	to	25 September 1992

Venus exalted in Pisces:

28 February 1989	to	23 March 1989
7 April 1990	to	4 May 1990
30 January 1991	to	22 February 1991
14 March 1992	to	7 April 1992
4 January 1993	to	2 February 1993

Venus debilitated in Virgo:

5 October 1988	to	29 October 1988
25 July 1989	to	18 August 1989

8 September 1990	to	1 October 1990
12 July 1991	to	21 August 1991
8 August 1992	to	31 August 1992

Mars

Mars is strong in Aries and Scorpio, which it rules, exalted in Capricorn, and debilitated in Pisces. When Mars is favourably placed it improves the health of the brain and the eyes, nose and mouth, the bladder and urethra, the male reproductive organs, and stimulates potency. It likewise enlivens and energizes, gives greater courage and confidence, and boosts the ego. And while it encourages risk-taking, it protects those who take them from harm. It is similarly helpful to people who work in Mars-ruled professions, such as the army, the police, butchery, surgery, etc., or who work in industry. It is favourable for the buying of land and houses, weapons, products made of iron, four-legged animals, and minerals. Mars benefits travel to the south, improves relations with one's cousins and younger brothers, and gives success in all activities involving the use of fire.

Mars in Aries:

14 July 1988	to	23 October 1988
2 November 1988	to	19 January 1989
1 June 1990	to	12 July 1990
6 May 1992	to	14 June 1992

Mars in Scorpio:

5 November 1988	to	18 December 1988
17 October 1991	to	29 November 1991
28 September 1993	to	9 November 1993

Mars exalted in Capricorn:

30 January 1990	to	11 March 1990
10 January 1992	to	18 February 1992
21 December 1993	to	28 January 1993

Mars debilitated in Pisces:

24 October 1988	to	1 November 1988
21 April 1990	to	31 May 1990
29 March 1992	to	5 May 1992

Jupiter

Jupiter is strong in Sagittarius and Pisces, which it rules, exalted in Cancer, and debilitated in Capricorn. When Jupiter is well-placed by sign it benefits the health of the hips, thighs and the feet, and also lifts the spirits. It similarly helps study and learning, deepens one's religious feelings, and brings wealth and respect. Where relationships are concerned, Jupiter improves that between a wife and her husband, and also those with sons. It brings luck in banking and commerce, teaching, and in any involvement with government ministers and church officials. It is also favourable for those who cultivate fruit, travel in a north-easterly direction, collect money for charitable purposes, or who visit religious shrines.

During the coming five years Jupiter will not pass through either of the signs that it rules or through Capricorn, where it is debilitated. It will, however, travel through Cancer, where it is exalted, between 31 July 1989 and 18 August 1990. This will therefore be a very good period for those with Jupiter as the ruler of either their Sun sign or their rising sign.

Saturn

Saturn is strong in Capricorn and Aquarius, which it rules, exalted in Libra and debilitated in Aries. When Saturn is well-placed it benefits the health of the skin and the skeleton, hence it will speed up the healing of bones that have already been broken. It heightens ambition and helps in the attainment of a desired goal by increasing perseverance and determination. It likewise promotes guile and stealth. In specific terms, it benefits those who work in agriculture or who extract oil, coal, lead, etc. from the ground, or who work in kitchens, cemeteries, funeral parlours, scientific laboratories, collect rubbish, or who are trying to learn a foreign language. Lastly, it improves relations beween a master and his servants, favours travel in a westerly direction, and lengthens the life of those who are already old.

Saturn will not pass through either Libra, where it is exalted, or Aries, where it is debilitated, during the next five years, but it will consecutively travel through Capricorn and Aquarius, which will make the period a good one in the areas outlined above for those whom it rules.

Saturn in Capricorn:

13 November 1988   to   6 February 1991

Saturn in Aquarius:

7 February 1991   to   28 January 1994

7

MARITAL MATTERS

Star of love's soft interviews
Parted lovers on thee muse;
Their remembrancer in Heaven
Of thrilling vows thou art,
Too delicious to be riven
By absence from the heart.

From *To The Evening Star* by Thomas Campbell

If you are single you probably would like to know if you will one day get married, and if you do whether or not your union will be happy. In fact these are questions that are frequently asked of astrologers, which naturally suggests that marriage and the happiness expected from it are high on anyone's list of priorities.

But it does not require an astrologer to tell you that you will, in all likelihood, get married, because most people do. How happy the marriage makes you depends upon your choice of partner. If you select someone with whom you are compatible, it is likely to be; but if you don't, it probably won't be.

Unfortunately, however, we too often fall in love without really knowing the person concerned, only to find out later that we have made a mistake. Such risks are not taken in India, where it is usual for a prospective bridal couple to have their birth charts compared by a competent astrologer, who notes their harmonius and disharmonius points. If the former predominate, the marriage goes ahead; while if the latter are more in evidence, then it does not. Such arranged marriages are not, unlike ours, based on love, although love is a frequent result when two compatible people make their lives together.

The term *synastry* is used to describe the comparison of two birth charts, and is built up from the prefix *syn*, meaning 'together', and *aster*, or 'star'. It therefore means 'bringing the stars together', which is of course what the process is all about.

Synastry is a fairly complicated procedure. The Indian astrologer, for example, takes note of the position of the Moon in both charts, which can give a total of 36 harmonious points. If the charts display 18 or more harmonious points, the couple are considered to be generally compatible. He also evaluates the position of the Sun, Mars and Saturn, and the two nodes of the Moon, all of which are inherently malefic influences, in each chart. It is not favourable if these lie in the first, seventh or eighth house of either chart, or if they are placed in the second, fourth or twelfth house, although the latter positions are less threatening. However, if one of the planets mentioned is badly sited in both charts — if Mars, for instance, lies in the first house of one chart and the seventh house of the other — then the bad effects are neutralized, which is a point in favour for the couple concerned. Thus while a person might be judged a poor marriage prospect on the basis of his chart, he can form a satisfactory relationship with a like person due to the fact that the negativity of each is cancelled out — or, to put it another way, the individual weaknesses of character are turned into strengths when the couple are married.

Your rising sign is the point from which you can determine the type of person whom you are most likely to marry. Astrologers regard it as forming what is known as the first house of the chart, which signifies the sort of person that you are. The sign that lies seventh from it, which comprises the seventh house or the house of marriage, symbolizes the type of individual to whom you will be most strongly attracted — and with whom, therefore, you are most likely to tie the knot.

The following signs are seventh from one another:

Aries – Libra
Taurus – Scorpio
Gemini – Sagittarius
Cancer – Capricorn
Leo – Aquarius
Virgo – Pisces

Hence if you have an Aries ascendant, your marriage partner will probably be a Libra type, that is, who either has his (or her) Sun in Libra, or who has, and this is more probable, a Libra ascendant. And similarly, if you have Libra rising, your ideal marriage partner will have either Aries rising or his (or her) Sun in Aries.

Moreover, if you have Aries rising, which is a Fire sign, you are also quite compatible with someone who has either the Sun in one of the other Air signs, these being Gemini and Aquarius, or who has one of these signs rising. And likewise, if you have Libra rising, which is an Air sign, you are similarly compatible with a person who has the Sun in Leo or Sagittarius, the two other Fire signs, or who has either Leo or Sagittarius rising.

The three Earth signs are Taurus, Virgo and Capricorn, each of which, as the above table indicates, is most compatible with the Water sign lying seventh from it, and vice versa. But as with the Fire and Air sign types, each Earth sign individual is also quite compatible with the other two Water signs types, just as each Water sign type is compatible with the two other Earth sign types. Thus if you have, for example, a Scorpio ascendant, you are most compatible with someone who has either Taurus rising or the Sun in Taurus, although you could form a tolerably happy union with a person with either a Virgo or Capricorn ascendant or who has the Sun in one of these two signs.

Should you be a woman it is not favourable for you to have the Sun in the sign that is seventh from your rising sign, as this bodes ill in marital matters, suggesting as it does separation and possible divorce. Thus if you have, for example, Gemini rising and the Sun in Capricorn, then your marriage is likely to be difficult. This is particularly true if your rising sign is Aries and the Sun is placed in Libra, where it is debilitated. However, ths does not apply to those who have Aquarius rising and the Sun in Leo, as Leo is the Sun's own sign, or to those who have Libra rising and the Sun in Aries, where it is exalted. These two latter placements of the Sun turn its otherwise harmful seventh house effects into positive ones.

Similarly, if you have either Sagittarius rising or Pisces rising, the former placing Gemini, and the latter Virgo, in the seventh house, this is a strong indication of more than one marriage, Gemini being a double sign, while Virgo, ruled as it is by Mercury, has comparable double characteristics.

The position of Venus in a man's chart and Jupiter in a woman's chart is important, the former being the significator for a wife and the latter for a husband. If Venus is well-placed and well-aspected, it indicates that the man will find a compatible and loving wife, while if Jupiter is likewise well-situated in a woman's chart, then her husband will be all

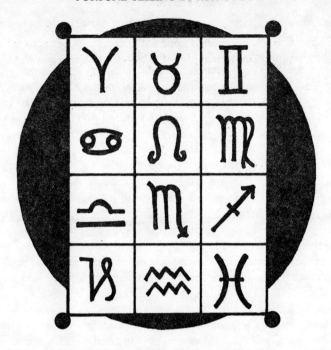

Figure 17

that she could ask for. But if the reverse is the case, it follows that the spouse will not be a suitable partner for the person concerned.

Your age of marriage can also be determined from your birth chart, although this is too technical a procedure to be considered here. However, you may find it fun to divine the month of your marriage from the oracle in Figure 17.

Strictly speaking, the oracle should be consulted in the evening during the hour of Venus, which is the third hour after sunset. If it is consulted at any other time the results cannot be guaranteed.

Sit at a table with the oracle in front of you, holding a new pin in your left hand. Next, close your eyes and think only of your hoped-for marriage and when it will be. Circle the pin three times around the oracle in a clockwise direction, then three times in an anti-clockwise direction and once in either a clockwise or an anti-clockwise direction. Then stab the pin on to the rectangle of 12 zodiac signs. The zodiac sign that you select indicates the month of your marriage. Hence if you land on

Aries you will marry between 21 March and 20 April, etc.

Should the pin come down outside the rectangle you are allowed two further attempts. This also applies if you strike the pin onto the black lines separating the squares. If you fail to prick the pin into one of the white squares on your third attempt, then you are unlikely ever to marry.

8

THE ASTROLOGICAL AGES

Glorious the sun in mid career;
Glorious th' assembled fires appear;
Glorious the comet's train:
Glorious the trumpet and alarm;
Glorious the Almighty's stretch'd-out arm;
Glorious th' enraptured main.

From *Song to David* by Christopher Smart

Ever since the cast of the musical *Hair* sang 'This is the dawning of the Age of Aquarius', it has become widely recognized that we are on the threshold of a new and brighter age, one during which mankind will put aside its racial and political hatreds and live in 'harmony and understanding'. But are these merely vain hopes or are there some good reasons for thinking that a more peaceful and loving era lies ahead? To answer this we must first define what an 'astrological age' is and examine the character of those that have ruled us during the last 10,000 years.

An astrological age takes its name from the zodiac sign in which the Sun is placed at the Vernal or Spring Equinox. At present the Sun is then located in Pisces, which tells us that we are living in the Age of Pisces. The length of the age is measured by the time it takes for the Equinox to move backwards or precede through the sign. We have reached the point when the Sun lies close to Beta Piscium, which marks the mouth of the south-west fish of the constellation Pisces, at the Spring Equinox. In a few years' time the Equinox will precede into Aquarius, which is when the Age of Aquarius will begin.

The precession of the Equinoxes is caused by the Earth wobbling on its axis, a movement that is itself brought about by the gravitational pull of the Sun and the Moon. The wobble is a slow and rather stately affair, the Equinoxes taking approximately 25,900 years to precede through the 12 zodiac signs, a length of time known as the Great Year.

If we divide 25,900 years by 12, we arrive at the time it takes for the Equinoxes (for both the Spring and the Autumn Equinox, and the two Solstices, are preceding through the zodiac) to move through any one sign, which is 2,158 years. This is therefore the length of an astrological age.

It was in about 140 BC, when the Sun was aligned with Gamma Arietis or Mesarthim at the Spring Equinox, that the Greek astronomer Hipparchus discovered that the Equinoxes were preceding. Not long afterwards, in about 100 BC, the Spring Equinox took place when the Sun had vacated Aries for Pisces, which is when the Age of Pisces commenced. Using this as our baseline, we can calculate that the Age of Aquarius will start in the year 2,058 AD. Similarly, by reckoning backwards, we can likewise determine that the Age of Aries started in the year 2,258 BC. The Age of Aries was in turn preceded by the Age of Taurus (c. 4,416 – 2,258 BC), the Age of Taurus by the Age of Gemini (c. 6,574 – 4,416 BC), the Age of Gemini by the Age of Cancer (c. 8,732 – 6,574BC), and the Age of Cancer by the Age of Leo (c. 10,890 – 8,732 BC). Hence since the end of the last Ice Age, which terminated, appropriately enough, in the Age of Leo, and the start of the present Age of Pisces, there have been five astrological ages: Leo, Cancer, Gemini, Taurus and Aries. And during each, so it is claimed, the character of the zodiac sign in question has imposed itself upon both the world in general and the activities of man.

This is extremely interesting in view of the fact that the ancient Greeks believed that there had been five races of men, of which they were the last and most degenerate of all. The poet Hesiod, who wrote in about 700 BC, long before the precession of the Equinoxes had been discovered and the idea of astrological ages formulated, gives a graphic account of these five races in his *Works and Days*. He tells us that:

The gods, who live on Mount Olympus, first
Fashioned a golden race of mortal men;
These lived in the reign of Cronos, king of heaven,
And like the gods they lived with happy hearts
Untouched by work or sorrow. Vile old age
Never appeared, but always lively-limbed,
Far from all ills, they feasted happily.

These fortunate people were eventually and unaccountably 'hidden in the ground'. To replace them the gods 'fashioned a lesser, silver race of men', who, because they 'injured one another and forsook the gods', were supplanted by a 'race of bronze'. These were in turn succeeded by another brazen race, but 'more just and good, a godlike race of heroes', who were followed by the men of Hesiod's time, 'the race of iron'.

What is significant about these five races of men is that each can be matched with one or other of the five astrological ages mentioned above.

The Age of Leo corresponds to the period during which the golden race lived. After all, the planetary ruler of Leo is the Sun, whose metal is gold. It was during this age that the weather became warmer, which brought about a melting of the great ice sheets that covered most of the northern hemisphere.

The Age of Leo was followed by that of Cancer, the zodiac sign ruled by the Moon, whose metal is silver. This age hence corresponds to the time in which Hesiod's silver race lived. Cancer is also associated with water and the sea, and it was during this period, following on from the glacial melting, that the oceans as we know them today came into existence.

The succeeding Age of Gemini can be identified with that inhabited by Hesiod's first brazen race, who 'loved the groans and violence of war'. It was during this period, in about 6,000 BC, that copper was first used, the hot treatment of which led to the manufacture of bronze. And while quicksilver, the metal of Mercury, the ruler of Gemini, plays no part in bronze making, tin certainly does. Tin is the metal of Jupiter, the ruler of Sagittarius, the sign lying opposite to Gemini in the zodiac.

The following Age of Taurus corresponds to the period of time when Hesiod's second race of bronze existed. Taurus is ruled by Venus, whose metal is copper, the principal ingredient of bronze. The Age of Taurus began in 4,416 BC, which is when the hot treatment of copper was first employed, this rendering the metal less brittle. Bronze itself was invented in about 3,000 BC, during the second half of the Age of Taurus.

The ancient Greeks lived during the Age of Aries, the Ram. According to Hesiod they were part of the race of iron. Aries is ruled by Mars, whose metal is iron.

These ages accord in basic outline with the Three Age system of modern archaeology, that is, the Stone Age, Bronze Age and Iron Age, which are named after the principal material or metal used in the manufacture of tools and weapons. The Age of Leo and the Age of Cancer together comprise the archaeologist's Stone Age, when mankind lived in simple tribal groups and survived by hunting and gathering. 'Ungrudgingly,' says Hesiod, and perhaps accurately, 'the fertile land gave up her fruits unasked. Happy to be at peace, they lived with every want supplied.' Similarly, the Age of Gemini and the Age of Taurus together form the archaeologist's Bronze Age, while the Age of Aries corresponds to the Iron Age.

It was during the Age of Gemini, which lasted from about 6,574 BC to 4,416 BC, that mankind took its first faltering steps towards what we would call 'civilized' life. Metalworking began, which led to the use of copper for the manufacture of weapons and ornaments like brooches and armbands, trade between different tribal groups was established, which resulted, naturally enough, in increasing conflict, and animal husbandry — the keeping of cattle, sheep and goats — was practised. Hence it comes as no surprise to learn that the Greeks regarded Mercury (or Hermes) as the god of metal-working, trade and commerce, and herds and flocks.

Taurus, the Bull, an Earth sign, is traditionally associated with agriculture and rural life. And it was during the Age of Taurus, which began in about 4,416 BC and lasted until about 2,258 BC, that the first settlements were established on the banks of the Tigris and Euphrates rivers and, later, the Egyptian Nile. In Sumer, as already discussed, cities were built of baked brick, agriculture was developed, and a leisured class had both the time and the interest to be artistically creative. And these activities — building, farming and art — are typically Taurean. Both the Mesopotamian and the Egyptian civilizations were dependent upon either irrigation or flooding, which allowed them to cultivate an otherwise parched earth. And in the zodiac, the sign lying opposite to Taurus is Scorpio, a Water sign.

Bull worship was likewise common during this period. Enlil, or Lord Air, who formed part of the Sumerian supreme triad and who was worshipped as a patron of the earth, was often portrayed in the form of a bull or as riding upon a bull. In Egypt the ancient deity Ptah, who was the third most important of the gods, responsible as he was for temple construction, metalworking and art, was said to have been reincarnated as the divine bull Apis. In fact a live bull, distinguished by certain markings, such as a white triangle on its forehead and a crescent moon on its right flank, was kept at Memphis, and the future divined from its movements. Egyptian archaeological digs have turned up many mummified bulls, which had evidently been buried with great ceremony in splendid sarcophagi.

The Age of Taurus, characterized as much by building as by agriculture, was suitably terminated by the construction of the largest pyramids, notably the Great Pyramid at Giza, which was built by Khufu or Cheops.

The Age of Aries, which started in about 2,258 BC, saw the eventual eclipse of the old earth-water civilizations and the emergence of diverse, warlike groups. It became a peculiarly martial period, due mainly to the fact that population pressures caused mass migrations, which brought different peoples into conflict. Hardly surprisingly, the age culminated in the rise of the Roman Empire.

As might be expected from the astrological infusion of Martian energy, the Age of Aries was a formative one for mankind. It has already been noted how the Akkadian hegemony over the cities of the Tigris and Euphrates valleys was broken by internal revolution and by foreign invasion, and while this resulted in a short-lived Sumerian renaissance, during which the famous ziqqurats were built, the outside pressures were too powerful to withstand. Indeed, in 2006 BC Ur itself was sacked by the Elamites and the Sumerian and Akkadian empires overthrown.

Egypt was similarly invaded by the Hyksos in about 1,900 BC and was to remain in their power for almost two hundred years. Yet even after they had been defeated and chased out of Egypt, the threat of foreign invasion remained, the Pharaohs having to mount campaigns against the Hittites, the Sea Peoples, the Libyans, and the Assyrians. But finally, however, Egypt was again conquered, by the Romans.

Iron working was mastered in about 1,500 BC by the Hittites, who established an empire in Asia Minor that lasted until 1,225 BC. They carefully kept the secret of iron smelting to themselves until their downfall, when it spread rapidly, giving to those who learned it a distinct military advantage, iron weapons being greatly superior to those made of bronze. This was when the Iron Age of the archaeologists began, and when Hesiod's 'race of iron' had its birth. Indeed, the poet lamented:

> I wish I were not of this race, that I
> Had died before, or had not yet been born.
> This is the race of iron. Now, by day,
> Men work and grieve unceasingly; by night,
> They waste away and die.

Yet the radical changes that took place during the Age of Aries had a stimulating effect on men's minds. The period saw the beginning of science and philosophy, and important advances were made in mathematics, geometry, astronomy and geography.

These progressive steps were largely taken by the Greeks, who perhaps best represent the individual spirit of the age. In the proto-Greek period the bull cults were suppressed, and Zeus, a sky god, was established as the supreme deity of the Greek pantheon. And while Zeus was said to have been suckled by a goat as an infant and wore a goat-skin aegis, his sacred animal was the ram, whose form he took on several occasions, such as when Olympus was attacked by the monster Typhon. Aries is, of course, the sign of the Ram, and is closely identified with individuality and with the ego or self. Hence is it perhaps not surprising that the Greeks hated tyranny and favoured democracy, which allows individual participation in the running of a state.

Much of the Age of Aries' personality can be ascribed to the fact that Libra, which is ruled by Venus, lies opposite to Aries in the zodiac, the tension between Mars and Venus producing the destructive and constructive features of the age.

Yet it was the Romans and their culture that became the crowning expression of the Age of Aries. They defeated their main Mediterranean rivals, the Cathaginians, in 146 BC and from that moment on were free to found their empire, which at its maximum extent stretched from Britain in the far north-west to Armenia in the distant east. Rome brought order, discipline and the rule of law to her largely barbaric neighbours, and the European provinces that she founded, like Lusitania, Tarraconensis and Belgica, exist today as the modern states into which they developed. In fact it wasn't until Julius Caesar (who was born in 100 BC at the start of the Age of Pisces) crossed the Rubicon and precipitated a civil war, that Rome became an autocracy and acquired the empire with which we are familiar. One of Julius Caesar's first acts on gaining supreme power was to reorganize the calendar. Suetonius tells us that 'he linked the year to the course of the Sun by lengthening it from 355 days to 365, abolishing the short extra month intercalated after every second February, and adding an entire day every fourth year.'

The Roman Empire was the springboard for the Age of Pisces, whose character is embodied in the birth of Jesus Christ, who came to bestride both it and the world like a colossus. For Jesus became a fisher of men; his 12 disciples were all fishermen, and his symbol is the fish.

The Age of Pisces has been distinguished, at least until the last century, by a preoccupation with religion and with things of the spirit. The spread of Christianity in the West was paralleled by that of Islam in the Middle East and Buddhism in the East. In its early centuries it saw the defeat of the Romans by barbarian invaders from the north (from damp, foggy Piscean parts), which resulted in a long retreat into the ignorance and superstition of the Dark Ages (Pisces is an introverted sign). Later, the European awakening of the Renaissance led to a period of maritime expansion and the discovery of the New World, which reached its zenith in the nineteenth century when England, Germany, France, Holland, etc. founded vast overseas empires.

We are now living at the tail-end of that age. Its energies are running down and fading away, leading as it has to increasing disorder and confusion. Our era has already experienced two World Wars and a host of smaller ones, and few parts of the world are untouched by violence of some kind. It is little wonder, therefore, that many people are looking forward with hopeful hearts to the coming Age of Aquarius, with its promise of peace, harmony and understanding.

The Age of Aquarius will start, give or take a few years, in 2058 AD. Aquarius, the Water-Carrier, is a Fixed Air sign. Its traditional planetary ruler is Saturn, whose metal is lead, while its modern planetary ruler is Uranus, whose metal is uranium. Aquarians are known for their stubborn independence, their Utopian idealism, their love of change, and their interest in science and technology. Yet they are also humanitarians, and they like to see others treated fairly and justly. Aquarius has also been called the sign of genius. Indeed, studies have shown that the majority of intellectual leaders — writers, scientists and philosophers — were born with the Sun placed in the sign.

Because the character of a zodiac sign impresses itself upon the age that it rules, this suggests that the Age of Aquarius will be notable for the following things: one, a rapid expansion of scientific research and its technological application, a development that is already underway; two, an increasing dependence on nuclear energy, which uses the two Aquarian metals, lead and uranium; three, greater freedom for those living under totalitarian regimes, with the most significant changes occurring in the Soviet Union, which is ruled by Aquarius; and four, a raised intellectual level for the human race as a whole, which will be brought about by better education and by the birth of more able people. These changes will necessarily result in increased international co-operation and, in time, to a more peaceful and humane world.

However, we should not expect an immediate end to strife and war, although what changes that do take place will probably happen suddenly and unexpectedly. The Age of Aquarius has not yet begun, but when it does it will last for over two thousand years. It takes time for the energies of any age to manifest, although the first 150 years seem to be peculiarly significant. After all, the Age of Pisces brought about the rise of the Roman Empire and the birth of the Messiah in its early stages, which indicates that the Age of Aquarius may begin equally momentously.

If so, we may be on the brink of a genuine new age, one during which mankind will turn away from the pursuit of money and power and instead open its heart to the infinitely more precious gifts of the spirit.

9

THE STAR IN THE EAST

O star of wonder, star of night,
Star with royal beauty bright,
Westward leading, still proceeding,
Guide us to thy perfect light.

Refrain of *We Three Kings* by John Henry Hopkins

Almost two thousand years ago, quite soon after the start of the Age of Pisces, an event took place, that while quite ordinary in itself, was to change the world. For in a stable in the little town of Bethlehem, in Judaea, a young woman named Mary gave birth to a son. She called him Yeshu, or Jesus. Later, he was given the title *Christos*, meaning 'the anointed one'. And thus it was that Jesus Christ, the Messiah, came into the world.

St Matthew tells us that Jesus' birth was accompanied by the appearance of an unusual star, which brought three 'wise men' to Jerusalem in search of him, asking: 'Where is he that is born King of the Jews? for we have seen his star in the east, and are come to worship him.'

This naturally raises questions as to what the star was and why it suggested to the visitors that someone very special had been born in Israel. Moreover, if we can satisfactorily identify the star, it may be possible to date accurately the birth of Jesus.

But surely, you may object, we already know the date of Jesus' birth: he came into the world on 25 December 1 AD. After all, don't we celebrate Christ's birthday on 25 December and date our years from that of his birth, 1 AD?

Yes, we do. But unfortunately the man who was given the job of determining the year of Jesus' birth made a mistake, while 25 December was stolen from the followers of Mithras, whose cult was early Christianity's chief rival, who regarded it as their holy day, when the Sun was reborn.

At the time of Jesus' birth Israel or, more properly, Palestine, was a Roman province, ruled by Herod the Great. And the Romans, following the example set by the Greeks, who dated their years from the first Olympiad (776 BC), dated theirs from the founding of Rome, which took place, by our reckoning, in 753 BC. The Romans called this date *Anno Urbis Conditae*, which means 'the year of the founding of the city'. Anno Urbis Conditae was abbreviated to AUC, and therefore Rome was founded, as far as the Romans were concerned, in 1 AUC. Similarly, Hannibal was defeated in 553 AUC and Julius Caesar was assassinated in 710 AUC.

The Roman system of dating was employed throughout their empire and was obviously not changed at the time when Jesus was born. Indeed, it was not until several centuries later, when Christianity had superseded paganism, that the leaders of the Church decided to date the Christian era from Jesus' birth. In 553 AD they asked a Syrian monk named Dionysus Exiguus to determine exactly when Jesus was born, and by consulting what records were available to him he came to the conclusion that this had happened in 754 AUC. This date was then changed to 1 AD — AD being the abbreviation of *Anno Domini*, which means 'the year of our Lord'.

Now St Matthew tells us that 'Jesus was born in Bethlehem of Judaea in the days of Herod the king'. But unfortunately, we know that King Herod died in 750 AUC — that is, four years *before* the date calculated by Dionysus for Jesus' birth. According to our dating system Herod died in 4 BC and as tradition is quite clear on the point that Jesus was born while Herod was still alive, he could not have been born later than this date. We are thus left in the uncomfortable position of having to agree that Jesus was born well before the official year of his birth (1 AD).

We know from the writings of the Jewish historian Josephus that Herod died before the next passover occurred, which happened on 1í determined that this took place on 13 March 4 BC. We also know that Herod died before the next passover occured, which happened on 11 April of that year, which naturally places his death sometime between those two dates. It also means that the birth of Jesus could not have happened later than 11 April 4 BC.

But there is no reason to think that Jesus was born immediately before Herod died. St Matthew tells us that Herod asked the wise men to seek Jesus out and then report back to him, so that he could 'worship him also'. The wise men, however, upon finding Jesus and presenting to him their gifts of gold, frankincense and myrrh, were warned 'in a dream that they should not return to Herod, (and) they departed into their own country another way'. Joseph, the father of Jesus, subsequently had a dream in which an angel appeared and told him, 'Arise, and take the young child and his mother, and flee into Egypt'. This Joseph did, leaving behind a very angry and frustrated Herod, who 'slew all the children that were in Bethlehem, and in all the coasts thereof, from two years old and under, according to the time which he had diligently enquired of the wise men'. We are also told that Joseph, Mary and Jesus remained in Egypt until Herod died.

Furthermore, we know from Josephus — who does not, by the way, mention the massacre of the infants — that Herod was afflicted with a painful and debilitating illness, which produced 'an unbearable itching all over the body, constant pains in the lower bowel, swellings on the feet as in dropsy, inflammation of the abdomen, and mortification of the genitals, producing worms; as well as difficulty in breathing, especially when lying down, and spasms in all his limbs'. This led Herod to visit the hot baths at Callirrhoe, which lies some 60 miles from Jerusalem, on the other side of the Dead Sea, for treatment before he died. And when he was returning to Jerusalem, he stopped for an unknown time at Jericho, where — and this may be the event that gave rise to the story of the massacre of the infants — he arranged for 'the most eminent men of every village in the whole of Judaea' to be locked up in the Hippo-drome, ordering his sister Salome, 'As soon as I die, kill them all — let loose the soldiers amongst them: then all Judaea and every family will weep for me — they can't help it'.

All these various happenings suggest that a period of at least several weeks went by, although probably a lot longer period of time, between the birth of Jesus and Herod's death, which means that Jesus' birth must be pushed back to 5 BC or before.

The three 'wise men', whose traditional names are Caspar, Melchior and Balthazar and who came 'from the east to Jerusalem', were almost certainly Chaldean astrologers or Magi, despite the fact that they are also referred to as 'kings'. This being so, we can say that they witnessed a bright celestial object, the so-called Star of Bethlehem, in Mesopotamia and interpreted it as a sign that a 'King of the Jews' had been born in Palestine.

But where did they make their observations, what did they see and why did they interpret it as they did?

It is known that there was a famous school of astrology at the Mesopotamian town of Sippur, at which, interestingly enough, many Jews studied. The cuneiform tablets on which the astrologers there recorded their observations have been discovered, and these have shown that in 7 BC they watched a conjunction of Jupiter and Saturn with great interest. The conjunction was unusual in that the two planets actually conjoined three times during the six-month period from May to December, 7 BC.

The ancients did not know that Jupiter, Saturn and the other planets are solid bodies without light of their own. They believed them to be special kinds of stars, having as they do the apparent power of independent movement, and so it would not have been unusual for the Magi to refer to a 'star' when what they were actually talking about was a planetary conjunction.

What was special about this conjunction was that the Jews regarded Saturn, which they called Kiyun, as the protector of Israel, most particularly as it is the ruler of Saturday, their Sabbath, while Jupiter, which they regarded as the ruler of Sunday, was linked with both kingship and divine revelation. Furthemore, the conjunction took place in Pisces, which was the zodiac sign thought to favourably influence Israel. Hence such a conjunction, occurring as it did in Pisces, could reasonably be interpreted as announcing the birth of a 'King of the Jews' by Chaldean astrologers who were familiar with Jewish astrological ideas, as those of Sippur would have been.

Modern astronomers have calculated that Jupiter and Saturn first conjoined at 21 degrees Pisces on 29 May 7 BC. At that time of the year the conjunction would only have been visible at sunrise for about two hours. But more importantly, it would have appeared in the sky to the east of Sippur. This accords with what the three wise men said to Herod: 'Where is he that is born King of the Jews? for we have seen his star in the east, and are come to worship him.'

As Jupiter 'passed' Saturn, which had begun to retrograde (or move 'backwards' in the sky), the two planets moved out of conjunction and separated. But then Jupiter itself went retrograde, caught up with the already retrograding Saturn, and the two planets again conjoined on 3 October 7 BC. There is good reason to think that it was this second conjunction that prompted the Magi to set out on their journey to Jerusalem. For not only would it have been uncomfortably hot to travel such a distance earlier in the year, but they would have known by mathematical calculation that a third conjunction was going to take place, which would give them the opportunity to time their arrival in Jerusalem when it happened.

Indeed, we know from St Matthew that 'the star, which they saw in the east, went before them, till it came and stood over where the young child was'. This implies that the star moved from the east to the west, which was the direction in which the Magi travelled as they journeyed from Sippur to Jerusalem. And this is what would have happened if the conjunction under discussion was the 'star' of Bethlehem. (It is ironic, however, that the conjunction of Jupiter and Saturn was seemingly ignored by the Jews themselves, yet prompted a long overland journey by camel for three 'wise men' from the east.) As the year progresses the constellations shift from east to west, so that while Pisces lay in the east in May, 7 BC, it would be placed in the west by the time 4 December came around, which was when the third and most significant conjunction of Jupiter and Saturn occurred.

We can therefore envisage the Magi as having made their first observation of the 'star' of Bethlehem on or around 29 May 7 BC, setting off on their journey to Jerusalem (probably by camel) in early October, after witnessing the second conjunction, and reaching their destination a little before the third conjunction, which accords with St Matthew, who says: 'When they heard the king, they departed; and lo, the star, which they saw in the east, went before them, till it came and stood over where the young child was.' By December of that year the constellation of Pisces was well in the west, and the conjunction was produced by Jupiter and Saturn aligning at 16 degrees Pisces. We can therefore postulate that the three wise men reached the stable 'where the young child was' on the date that the two planets came into full conjunction, that is, on 4 December 7 BC.

However, we do not know how old Jesus was when that happened. All St Matthew tells us is that the wise men, on finding the place where the holy family was, 'saw the young child with Mary his mother, and fell down, and worshipped him.' It is impossible to tell from this whether or not Jesus was new born, a few days old, a few weeks old, or even a few months old. Yet St Luke gives a clue when he reports that at the time Jesus was born 'there were in the same country shepherds abiding in the field, keeping watch over their flock by night.' As it is too wet and chilly to put sheep out to pasture at night in the Holy Land in November and December, this could mean that Jesus was born in the October of 7 BC.

He would therefore have been between one and two months old when the Magi found him. But all we can safely conclude is that Jesus was born in 7 BC, sometime before 4 December.

INDEX